Scout, Atticus, and Boo

Mary McDonagh Murphy is an Emmy Award-winning producer and an independent documentary director. This book is based on her interviews for the film *Hey, Boo: Harper Lee and To Kill a Mockingbird*, released theatrically and broadcast on PBS's *American Masters*. She has written for *Newsweek*, the *Chicago Tribune*, the *New York Post*, and *Publishers Weekly*. She lives in Scarborough, New York, with her husband, Bob Minzesheimer, and their two children.

Scout, Atticus, and Boo

A CELEBRATION OF
To Kill a Mockingbird

MARY McDONAGH MURPHY

arrow books

1 3 5 7 9 10 8 6 4 2

Arrow Books
20 Vauxhall Bridge Road
London SW1V 2SA

Arrow Books is part of the Penguin Random House group of companies
whose addresses can be found at global.penguinrandomhouse.com.

Penguin
Random House
UK

First published by Harper Collins in 2010
First published by Arrow Books 2015

www.randomhouse.co.uk

A CIP catalogue record for this book is
available from the British Library.

ISBN 9781784753054

Printed and bound by CPI Group (UK) Ltd, Croydon, CR0 4YY

To the memory of Constance Laibe Hays,
a true friend and a good writer

&

for Bob, Kate, and James Minzesheimer,
the three best things that have ever happened to me

Contents

Foreword:

A Mockingbird Mosaic

BY WALLY LAMB

During the summer of 1992, when my first novel, *She's Come Undone*, was published, I'd drive my sons, ages eleven and seven, to the local shopping mall and, approaching the bookstore, offer them a deal, "Whoever's the first to find Dad's book on the shelf gets fifty cents." They'd dash into the store. I'd wait. And wait. And wait some more. Eventually the boys would return, slump-shouldered and pouty-faced. "We give up, Dad," they'd say. "Can we still have the money?" Five years later, Oprah Winfrey held up a copy of *Undone* and announced to her millions of viewers that it was the latest selection of her wildly popular book club. The following week the novel was number one. A *Boston Globe* article captures the moment. Above a photo of me seated before a high school class, a deer-in-the-headlights expression on my face, a headline asks, "Wally *WHO*?"

I own three copies of *To Kill a Mockingbird*. One is a lush leather-bound edition with gilt-edged pages—a gift from a bookseller for whom I'd signed some first editions of my novels. The second copy was a present from my publisher—a fortieth anniversary edition that brought tears to my eyes when I opened it, leafed to the title page, and saw Lee's signature. My third copy, the oldest and sorriest of the three, is the one I hold most dear. The cover's long gone. The pages are foxed, the margins filled with my scrawled notes. Within the text, certain words—*ambidextrous, florid, primeval*—are circled and flagged for vocabulary lessons. This is my teaching copy of the Popular Library paperback, circa 1974, when *Mockingbird*, like some of my students, was fourteen years old. The price of the book: a buck and a quarter. The paperback printing number: 94. (The original hardcover published by J. B. Lippincott had returned to press twenty-two times before that.) The binding of this copy fell apart decades ago, and so the loose pages are held together with a black-and-silver metal clip large enough to set off airport security alarms. Said pages have been shuffled hopelessly out of sequence. Thus, Scout walks Boo Radley back to his house *before* Atticus discredits Bob Ewell on the witness stand. That cranky old racist Mrs. Dubose dies drug-free *before* Jem is obliged to read to her as she painfully withdraws from morphine. And, this is strange, the final metal-clipped pages of my tattered teaching copy have wandered over from an entirely different book: Mark Twain's *The Adventures of Huckleberry Finn*. Strange but fitting, I guess. In terms of literary heritage, I think of Salinger's *The Catcher in the Rye* as *Mockingbird*'s older brother and *Huckleberry Finn* as the father of both books. All three novels, each a product of its era, give voice to outsider American kids trying to negotiate an adult world full of hypocrites. All three counterbalance the pain of human failings with the healing balm of humor. "Persons attempting to find a motive in this narrative will be prosecuted," Twain warns before he allows Huck to speak. "Persons attempting to find a moral in it will be banished; persons attempting to find a plot in it will be shot." I can all but hear the droll, self-effacing Nelle Harper Lee chuckling at Sam Clemens's tongue-in-cheek "warning."

I met documentary filmmaker Mary Murphy the day she arrived at my Connecticut home to interview me about *Mockingbird*. As her two-man crew, cameraman Rich White and sound engineer Jack Norflus, converted my garage into a makeshift television studio, Mary and I chatted about our kids, our musical tastes, good New York restaurants. But once the mic had been clipped to my shirt and the bright lights were aimed at my world-weary mug, our conversation shifted to my long-standing relationship with Harper Lee's only novel—first as a reluctant teenage reader; then as a teacher of high school, university, and prison students; then as a fiction writer; and finally as a writer who, like Lee, was taken unawares by best-sellerdom. At the end of the interview, Mary and the guys backed down my driveway and, over the next several years, drove on to the homes and offices of twenty-something other interviewees. Recently, when I received an advance copy of *Scout, Atticus, and Boo: A Celebration of "To Kill a Mockingbird,"* the companion book to Murphy's illuminating documentary, I flipped past my own comments and hungrily read the interviews of others: writers, teachers, celebrities, and those who know Harper Lee and/or Maycomb, a.k.a. Monroeville, the Alabama town in which Lee was raised. "Each time another person agreed to be interviewed, I wondered if there was anything new to be said," Murphy writes. "Invariably, there was."

And how!

Attorney/author Scott Turow and TV's Tom Brokaw laud Harper Lee's bravery in writing *Mockingbird*, given the tenor of the times and the fact that she was raised in the segregated South. "I think [Lee] helped liberate white people with that book," Brokaw says. James McBride, author of *The Color of Water: A Black Man's Tribute to His White Mother*, calls Lee "a brilliant writer," but stops short of calling her brave. He wonders why the book's black characters, heroic as they are, don't survive, and why there are no details about the life of the Finches' housekeeper, Calpurnia, after she goes home from work. "I think Martin Luther King was brave, Malcolm X was brave, James Baldwin, who was gay and black in America and who had to move to France was brave," he says. "I think she did the best she could, given how she was raised. That still doesn't absolve the book or this country of the whole business of racism." Novelist and fellow Monroeville native Mark Childress, Lee's junior by more than thirty years, nevertheless remembers the separate white and black service windows in the Dairy Queen of his youth. Educator Mary Tucker, who taught in the public schools of Lee's hometown before and after segregation, recalls the era in which, as a black woman shopping for clothes in downtown Monroeville, she was obliged to try on dresses over her own clothes—something white shoppers were not obliged to do. Of the "hard scrabble" time and place in which Harper Lee set her novel, the Reverend Thomas Lane Butts, pastor emeritus of the Methodist church where the Lee family worshipped, says, "It was a time in which black people were treated terribly and people took in racism with their mother's milk." Reverend Butts identifies Harper Lee as a "ministerial friend" and Lee's older sister, Alice Finch Lee, as one of his idols. In *Scout, Atticus, and Boo*, Mary Murphy includes her interview with ninety-eight-year-old Miss Alice, and it's a fascinating one.

Fascinating, too, is the discovery that Murphy's interviewees pledge their allegiance to several different characters. Feminist writers Anna Quindlen, Lee Smith, and Adriana Trigiani are lifetime members of the Scout Finch fan club. But bestselling novelist James Patterson identifies more with Scout's big brother. "My connection was more to Jem because he was a boy," he told Murphy. (I suppose Jem Finch's impact has leeched into my bones, too. To this day, whenever I write about jewels, spell check has to remind me that the word is "gems," not "jems.") The allegiances of attorney and author Scott Turow and lifelong civil rights activist Andrew Young lie with Atticus. "He is a paragon beyond paragons," Turow says. Young likens Tom Robinson's courtroom defender to the Eisenhower-appointed judges who took on the segregationists. "These were all the Southern intelligentsia—and they were Atticus Finch," Young observes. "They were the fine, upstanding men of wisdom and courage that really, without them we would not have had a civil rights movement." Novelist Richard Russo and singer Rosanne Cash are Atticus fans, too—more for his parenting than his lawyering.

In the pages ahead, you will read a fascinating mosaic: how and why the interviewees relate to *Mockingbird* and its characters, their varying reactions to the 1962 film based on the book, and their multitude of theories as to why Harper Lee never published another novel.

Here's mine.

Several years back, Harper Lee and Oprah Winfrey met for lunch in New York. The talk-show host's hope was that she might be able to convince Lee to be interviewed on her TV show. (Lee has consistently declined interviews since the mid-1960s.) In trying to let Oprah down easily, Lee said, "You know the character Boo Radley? Well, if you know Boo, then you understand why I wouldn't be doing an interview, because I am really Boo." But Boo was a recluse and Harper Lee, from all reports, is not. Lee is cagey and Boo was not. So if Lee is part Boo, I think she is also, on her own behalf, the novel's kind and cagey Sheriff Tate. In telling

Atticus why the "official" version of how Bob Ewell got killed will stray from what really happened, Sheriff Tate says, "To my way of thinkin', Mr. Finch, taking the one man who's done you and this town a great service an' draggin' him with his shy ways into the limelight—to me, that's a sin." A few sentences later, Scout likens the exposure of Boo to Maycomb's hero worship to "shootin' a mockingbird." So to *my* way of thinkin', the wise and wonderful Harper Lee is, simultaneously, Boo, Scout, the sheriff, and the mockingbird. She may not grant interviews, but she is still singing away via her 1960 masterpiece.

Finally, the teacher in me cannot resist giving you an assignment—albeit one that's sure to bring you hours and hours of pleasure. Read Mary Murphy's *Scout, Atticus, and Boo: A Celebration of "To Kill a Mockingbird"* or watch her documentary. Then watch the Robert Mulligan–directed theatrical film, adapted by playwright Horton Foote and starring Gregory Peck in his Oscar-winning role as Atticus Finch. Then go back, read, and savor the fifty-year-old original. Shuffle the above order as you desire. But however you choose to tackle this assignment, I invite you to think, feel, and enjoy.

Scout, Atticus, and Boo

PART I

Scout, Atticus, and Boo

Reading *To Kill a Mockingbird* is something millions of us have in common, yet there is nothing common about the experience. It is usually an extraordinary one. *To Kill a Mockingbird* leaves a mark. And somehow, it is hermetically sealed in our brains—the memory of it fresh and clear no matter how many decades have passed. If you ask, people will tell you exactly where they were and what was happening to them when they read Harper Lee's first and only novel. It may be the first "adult" book we read, assigned in eighth or ninth grade. Often it is the first time a young reader is completely kidnapped by a novel, taken on an enthralling ride until the very end. After half a century, *To Kill a Mockingbird*'s staying power is remarkable: still a best seller, always at the top of lists of readers' favorites, far and away the most widely read book in high school.

"I think it is our national novel," Oprah Winfrey told me when I interviewed her for my documentary about *To Kill a Mockingbird*'s power and influence. "If there was a national novel award, this would be it for the United States. When I opened my school [for girls in South Africa], everybody wanted to know what we can bring and what can we give the girls. I asked everybody to bring their favorite book, and I would say we probably have a hundred copies of this book. Each person who brought the book wrote their own words to the girls about why they believe this book was an important book, and everybody says something different."

That's because almost everyone can relate to it—one way or another. Look at all the ground *To Kill a Mockingbird* covers: childhood, class, citizenship, conscience, race, justice, fatherhood, friendship, love, and loneliness. With all due respect to the wave of social-networking sites, applications, and abbreviations in which we are awash these days, I would like to point out that the community this fifty-year-old novel invites and enjoys is one of the greatest social networks of all time. Try saying "Boo Radley" to the person next to you on the bus. Or say "chiffarobe," as Mayella Ewell does. Mention Scout, Atticus, Jem, Mrs. Dubose, or Tom Robinson, and see where it takes you. People respond. They connect. Friendships form.

When I met Liz Tirrell, a screenwriter and documentary director, it did not take long to find out she could recite line after line from the book and the movie. We bonded over "Hey, Mr. Cunningham . . . I'm Jean Louise Finch. I go to school with Walter; he's your boy, ain't he?"

When Pulitzer Prize–winning historian Diane McWhorter was growing up in Birmingham, Alabama, she and her schoolmates recited the "Hey, Mr. Cunningham" lines and spoke Scout whenever possible. "Cecil Jacobs is a big wet hen," and "What in the Sam Hill are you doing?" and other imitations rang out at recess.

Anna Quindlen, the Pulitzer Prize–winning columnist and novelist, said she simply could not be friends with anyone who does not "get" Scout. "I remember someone telling me that they thought Scout was a peripheral character, and I was shocked out of my skin."

But then, I have another friend, a novelist who teaches fiction writing, who told me that when she mentioned *To Kill a Mocking-*

bird as a favorite, a fellow professor said, "We don't consider that literature here."

Really?

"YOU HAVE ANOTHER THINK COMING"

That pronouncement sent me right back to the novel. And unlike other favorites from childhood, another reading of *To Kill a Mockingbird* rewards and reaffirms. The story is as rich as the Alabama soil it comes from; its veins can be mined over and over again. If you think you cannot go back to it and find more, "You have another think coming," as Scout Finch would say.

My second reading of *To Kill a Mockingbird* was a revelation. It felt as though I was reading it for the very first time. How could I have forgotten Calpurnia and "It's not necessary to tell all you know"? Or Dolphus Raymond, the drunk, who was not a drunk at all? Or all the history? And the writing. The writing! The economy was dazzling. My enthusiasm was unbridled, my appreciation immense.

Looking back, I see that the first time, I was blinded by love. For Scout: funny, smart, overall-wearing, fists-flying, lynch-mob-scattering Scout. Scout knew who she was, and she had the greatest father on the planet.

Here she was again—only better.

On her cousin: "Talking to Francis gave me the sensation of settling slowly to the bottom of the ocean. He was the most boring child I ever met."

On the neighbors: "The Radley Place was inhabited by an unknown entity the mere description of whom was enough to make us behave for days on end; Mrs. Dubose was plain hell."

On her father: "Atticus was feeble: he was nearly fifty."

On the caste system in her town: ". . . to my mind it worked this way: the older citizens, the present generation of people who had lived side by side for years and years, were utterly predictable to one another: they took for granted attitudes, character shadings, even gestures, as having been repeated in each generation and refined by time. Thus the dicta No Crawford Minds His Own Business, Every Third Merriweather Is Morbid, The Truth Is Not in the Delafields, All the Bufords Walk Like That, were simply guides to daily living."

After I finished, I carried my paperback copy of *To Kill a Mockingbird* around with me for weeks. I needed to stay in its thrall. I read random pages, sometimes aloud, and was instantly reinvigorated.

Novelist Mark Childress, who wrote *Crazy in Alabama*, told me he reads *To Kill a Mockingbird* "as a refresher course" almost every year. "Every time I go back, I'm impressed more by the simplicity of the prose. . . . Although it's plainly written from the point of view of an adult, looking back through a child's eyes, there's something beautifully innocent about the point of view, and yet it's very wise."

Allan Gurganus, author of *The Oldest Living Confederate Widow Tells All* and other novels, said of *his* rereading: "What's marvelous is that you see that sometimes the first things that happen to you are as big as they seemed. And, it's very moving to see what an evergreen and enduring achievement it's truly turned out to be."

"As Relevant Today as the Day It Was Written"

My second reading of *To Kill a Mockingbird* was fifteen years ago. And then, like Scout, I decided to go exploring. I began looking into the novel's history, stature, and popularity. By any measure, it is an astonishing phenomenon. An instant best seller, winner of the Pulitzer Prize, a screen adaptation ranked one of the best of all time. Fifty years after its publication, it sells nearly a million copies every year—hundreds of thousands more than *The Catcher in Rye*, *The Great Gatsby*, or *Of Mice and Men*, American classics that also are staples of high school classrooms.

No other twentieth-century American novel is more widely read. Even British librarians, who were polled in 2006 and asked, "Which book should every adult read before they die?" voted *To Kill a Mockingbird* number one. The Bible was number two. Why? What is it about this novel, I asked everyone I interviewed. "I think people want to read something substantial," answered novelist Lee Smith, author of *The Last Girls* and eleven other books. "They want to have something to believe in, and *To Kill a Mockingbird* manages to do that without being too preachy."

Until she retired from North Carolina State University, Smith taught *To Kill a Mockingbird* for twenty-five years. "Students are reading it today with the same responses we all had in the sixties," she said. "It still has a galvanizing effect on a young reader. This is a novel which *endures*, as opposed to other classics which don't appeal as much to readers today. *The Sun Also Rises* is a good example, because students just say, 'Who are all these people drinking in Spain? What is this about?' You never get that reaction to *To Kill a Mockingbird*. It remains as relevant today as it was the day it was written. It never ages. It's a story of maturing, certainly, and initiation, but told in such beautifully specific terms that it never seems generic."

Novelist Wally Lamb, author of *I Know This Much Is True* and *The Hour I First Believed*, told me he did not enjoy reading in high school. Then he found *To Kill a Mockingbird* in his sister's room. "I flipped it open and read the first couple of sentences and . . . two days later I, the pokiest reader I knew, had finished the book. It was the first time in my life that a book had captured me. That was exciting. I didn't realize that literature could do that." And when Lamb went on to teach high school in Connecticut, he saw his students respond the same way. "It was a book they read because they wanted to, not because they had to. It cast the same spell for my students as it had for me."

Winfrey was a young girl living with her mother in Milwaukee, Wisconsin, when a librarian recommended *To Kill a Mockingbird*. She remembered "just devouring it," and climbing right aboard the Scout bandwagon. "I wanted to be Scout, I thought I was Scout. I wanted an accent like Scout and a father like Atticus."

Who *doesn't* want a father like Atticus? Pulitzer Prize–winning novelist Richard Russo did. "Atticus Finch was the father maybe that I longed for," he said.

Beyond being an ideal father, Atticus Finch is a folk hero to lawyers. When Scott Turow, a lawyer who became famous for writing novels about lawyers, read *To Kill a Mockingbird* as a student in Chicago, "I promised myself that when I grew up and I was a man, I would try to do things just as good and noble as what Atticus had done for Tom Robinson."

Lest we forget, Atticus also is the best shot in the county. An understanding single father, an honest and humble lawyer, a respectful neighbor, Atticus is a paragon but never a caricature.

"People want to believe in an idealized world, and that has an instructive moral function," Turow said. "It's true that there aren't many human beings in the world like Atticus Finch—perhaps none—but that doesn't mean that it's not worth striving to be like him."

Boo Radley loomed large in all my conversations. The house, and the mystery and suspense built up around it, was familiar territory.

"Boo Radley cannot be overestimated as an important factor in this book," Smith said. "Every neighborhood has that house that's overgrown and those neighbors that are weird or that you never ever, ever see. And stories grow up about them. That figure always occupies a place in a child's imagination. And to demystify that—to make us see that people so radically different from us are OK, and can be helpful and wonderful—this is so important."

"Boo Radley is now a phrase in the language, [as in] the block's Boo Radley," said Gurganus. "Many people who haven't read *To Kill a Mockingbird* have that phrase in their lingo." Indeed, Boo Radley has entered not only our vernacular but also our yellow pages. Novelty stores, bars, and antiques dealers bear his name: Boo Radley's Store in Spokane; Boo Radley's Bar in Mobile, Boo Radley's Antiques in Los Angeles.

"I AM ALIVE, ALTHOUGH VERY QUIET"—HARPER LEE

All of this despite an author who has done nothing to publicize her book for more than forty-five years. In 1993, Harper Lee wrote to her agent, "Although *Mockingbird* will be thirty-three this year, it has never been out of print and I am still alive, although very quiet." The same can be said seventeen years later. Still among us, at eighty-four, Nelle Harper Lee, who dropped her first name when she published, was born in the small town of Monroeville, Alabama, and moved to New York around 1948. She has divided her time between the two cities ever since. In 1964, Lee gave an interview to Roy Newquist of WQXR, a New York radio station, and said she was working on a second novel "and it goes slowly, ever so slowly." Since then, she has not given another full interview or published another book, only adding to her mystique.

Reverend Thomas Lane Butts, the former pastor of Monroeville's First United Methodist Church, has been a friend of Lee's for more than twenty-five years. "Being famous and a celebrity is probably a lot of fun the first two or three months, but after you've been a celebrity for fifty years it gets old, I'm quite sure," he said. "She has controlled her own destiny. She doesn't have a PR person. She doesn't need one. I think she has led a happier life and certainly [a] more contented life because she has chosen how she has related to the public."

"It takes a kind of courage that almost nobody has in this country, where celebrity has replaced religion for a lot of people, to turn away from the church of publicity and say, 'I'm not going to pray there, I'm not going to appear there,'" Mark Childress said. "It's a kind of blasphemy in this society that she commits by refusing to participate in the publicity machine."

Occasionally, Lee has made public appearances, usually to pick up awards. In 2007, she was at the White House to receive the Presidential Medal of Freedom. Her picture has been taken, but she does not speak to the press. "A lot of people think that she's a recluse," said Reverend Butts, "and that is absolutely untrue. She's a person who enjoys her privacy like any other citizen would."

Albeit a citizen who wrote a book that has made—and continues to make—a difference to generations of readers. Oprah Winfrey once met Harper Lee for lunch in New York, hoping to coax the author onto her talk show. "I knew twenty minutes into the conversation that I would never be able to convince her to do an interview," she recalled. Nevertheless, "we were like instant girlfriends," she said. "It was just wonderful, and I loved being with her."

In 2002, Jon Meacham, the editor of *Newsweek* and Pulitzer Prize–winning biographer of Andrew Jackson, had a chance to talk with Lee when she accepted an honorary degree at the University of the South, in Sewanee, Tennessee, Meacham's alma mater. "I found her to be completely unassuming," he said, "and therefore all the more powerful for it."

Harper Lee, flanked by C-SPAN founder Brian Lamb and Ellen Johnson Sirleaf, the president of Liberia, recipients of the Presidential Medal of Freedom, November 5, 2007.

READING ALOUD

When I began filming interviews with writers and readers, I asked everyone to read aloud a favorite passage from the novel. In twenty-six interviews, only two passages were chosen more than once. Reverend Butts, Childress, Meacham, and Winfrey all chose the passage in which Atticus leaves the courtroom. He has lost the case but is honored in defeat by the black community relegated to the balcony. Scout is among them, and Reverend Sykes instructs her, "Miss Jean Louise, stand up. Your father's passing."

As she read, Oprah had tears in her eyes.

James McBride, the memoirist and novelist, and Rick Bragg, a Pulitzer Prize–winning reporter and memoirist, chose to read from the book's beginning:

When he was nearly thirteen, my brother Jem got his arm badly broken at the elbow. When it healed, and Jem's fears of never being able to play football were assuaged, he was seldom self-conscious about his injury. His left arm was somewhat shorter than his right; when he stood or walked, the back of his hand was at right angles to his body, his thumb parallel to his thigh. He couldn't have cared less, so long as he could pass and punt.

When enough years had gone by to enable us to look back on them, we sometimes discussed the events leading up to his accident. I maintain that the Ewells started it all, but Jem, who was four years my senior, said it started long before that. He said it began the summer Dill came to us, when Dill first gave us the idea of making Boo Radley come out.

McBride told me he read that passage repeatedly when he was writing his memoir, *The Color of Water: A Black Man's Tribute to His White Mother.* "This paragraph sets up the whole book," he said of Lee's opening. "It sets up the whole story. By speaking to the specific, the story of how her brother broke his arm, she speaks to the general problem of four hundred years of racism, slavery, socioeconomic classism, problems between classes, problems between people who have, people who don't, the courage of the working class, the isolation of the South, the identity crises of a young girl, and the coming out of a neighborhood recluse. All that in the story of her brother, who, when he was nearly thirteen, broke his arm."

McBride's memoir began, "When I was fourteen, my mother took up two new hobbies: riding a bicycle and playing the piano." I read that as an homage to the first sentence of *To Kill a Mockingbird.*

Bragg, who wrote *All Over but the Shoutin',* a tribute to *his* mother, grew up dirt-poor in Possum Trout, a tiny community in northern Alabama. He zeroed in on Lee's sentence "I maintain that the Ewells started it all, but Jem, who was four years my senior, said it started long before that." Bragg said, "Southern writers are always saying stuff to be profound, like *that's a quintessentially Southern phrase.* But the truth is, down here, everything started long before that. That's just the way it is."

DEEPER TRUTHS

Each time another person agreed to be interviewed, I wondered if there was anything new to be said. Invariably, there was.

"Stories that deal with injustice are really powerful [in America]," suggested novelist James Patterson, who lists *To Kill a Mock-ingbird* as one of the only two books he enjoyed reading during high school in Newburgh, New York. "I think we have more of a sense of that than they do in some places where injustice is more a fact of life."

Rosanne Cash, the singer/songwriter and memoirist, thought the novel should be read as a parenting manual: "There's just this beautiful naturalness that [Atticus] has and sense of confidence in his own skill as a parent. And respect for the child, that mutual respect."

To Kill a Mockingbird's small-town setting is what stuck with NBC's Tom Brokaw, who grew up in small towns throughout South Dakota and knew "not just the pressures that [Atticus] was under, but the magnifying glass that he lived in. This all takes place in a very small environment. People who live in big cities don't have any idea of what the pressures can be like in a small town when there's something controversial going on."

When Allan Gurganus read *To Kill a Mockingbird*, he "felt the permission to write about small-town life and the permission to feel that huge international drama, all the circumstances of truth, justice, and the American way, could be played out in a town of two thousand souls and could be played out by a single just man who stands up to be counted."

Meacham was impressed by the "moral ambiguity" of the novel's ending. "I think the courageous thing that Miss Lee did was end it on a tragic note. You would think in a novel like this, that's achieved this kind of status, it would be a very melodramatic tale of good and evil. Instead, it's a tale of good and evil that ends on a note of gray, which is where most of us live."

Historian McWhorter, who wrote *Carry Me Home: Birmingham, Alabama: The Climactic Battle of the Civil Rights Revolution*, said, "For a white person from the South to write a book like this in the late 1950s is really unusual—by its very existence an act of protest."

"It was an act of protest, but it was an act of humanity," said Andrew Young, the former UN ambassador, mayor of Atlanta, and veteran of the civil rights movement, who worked with Martin Luther King. "It was saying that we're not all like this. There are people who rise above their prejudices and even above the law."

Anna Quindlen, Lee Smith, and Adriana Trigiani, the novelist whose Big Stone Gap books are set in her Virginia hometown, all sang Scout's praises, each in a different verse. So did Lizzie Skurnick, who blogs about young adult books for Jezebel.com and is the author of *Shelf Discovery: The Teen Classics We Never Stopped Reading,* and David Kipen, former director of literature for the National Endowment for the Arts and supervisor of the NEA's Big Read program, which includes *To Kill a Mockingbird.*

I don't really give a rip about Atticus. He is fine, and he is a terrific dad. For me, this book is all about Scout. And I don't really care about anybody else in the book that much, except to the extent that they are nice to Scout and make life easier for Scout.

—ANNA QUINDLEN

Here's Scout, who believes in things, who is funny and curious and passionate and a tomboy. I think Scout has done more for Southern womanhood than any other character in literature.

—LEE SMITH

I craved the kind of life [Scout] had. She seemed to me to be fiercely independent; there seemed to be a streak of Pippi Longstocking in her, like she owned the town, and that appealed to me.

—ADRIANA TRIGIANI

Scout struggles with things in a very genuine way. The second half of the novel, those grand themes of justice, injustice, those are about how the world acts on us. But Scout is really about who we are in the world, how we decide that.

—LIZZIE SKURNICK

She's a scamp and hysterically funny, and no less funny as an adult looking back, although in a slightly more fermented and seasoned way. She's just great company.

—DAVID KIPEN

Richard Russo realized that the relationship between Scout and Atticus was burrowed deep within him. "It aided me in writing all of my father/daughter stuff, all my family stuff, because that is a quintessential American family, even though it's not typical."

As a young boy, Mark Childress read the novel on a porch in Monroeville, Alabama, where he, like Harper Lee, was born. "That was the first adult novel that I had ever read, and I was just about the age of Scout when I read it, and I was reading it in the setting where it happened. And it's the reason I'm a writer today. Something about seeing that ugly little town, which at that point had been sort of stripped of all of its charms, transformed into this magical thing that was in my hands."

Wally Lamb found *To Kill a Mockingbird* to be "a great course in how to write a novel." He pointed to Lee's "gorgeous" description of the town:

> *Maycomb was an old town, but it was a tired old town when I first knew it. In rainy weather the streets turned to red slop; grass grew*

on the sidewalks, the courthouse sagged in the square. Somehow it was hotter then: a black dog suffered on a summer's day; bony mules hitched to Hoover carts flicked flies in the sweltering shade of the live oaks on the square. Men's stiff collars wilted by nine in the morning. Ladies bathed before noon, after their three-o'clock naps, and by nightfall were like soft teacakes with frostings of sweat and sweet talcum.

Lamb said, "It is a one-paragraph course on writing, those tactile sensations, that's real writing. That's literature."

The "literature" question came up again, this time in the pages of the *New Yorker* in May 2006. In his review of *Mockingbird*, an unauthorized biography of Harper Lee by Charles Shields, Thomas Mallon dismissed Atticus as "a plaster saint" and Scout as "a highly constructed doll, feisty and cute on every subject from algebra to grown-ups." Mallon allowed that, "Indisputably, much in the novel works," but complained of "occasionally clumsy sentences," and also wrote that Horton Foote's screen adaptation was "rather better than the original material."

When I asked McWhorter about Mallon's essay, she responded directly to Mallon. "How many cities have read your books?" she asked.

McBride was even more exercised about Mallon's criticism. "Whoever this guy is, whatever this schmoo is, they're not going to be reading *his* book in fifty years. People are going to be reading Harper Lee in this country as long as they draw oxygen. It is a great book now, it was a great book yesterday, and it will be a great book tomorrow."

Scott Turow was perplexed. "I just think the grace of the writing is substantial, and I am confounded by people who attack it as a work of literature. I think it is a beautifully written and structured book. Is it sentimental? Yes, it's sentimental, but so was Steinbeck, and people still read Steinbeck."

Russo, a former professor at Colby College in Waterville, Maine, offered, "Back when I was teaching, I use to remind my students that masterpieces are masterpieces not because they are flawless but because they've tapped into something essential to us, at the heart of who we are and how we live."

By the time Mallon was asked if he would discuss any of this with me, his hate mail had piled up considerably. He said no, he was not going to be the skunk at that garden party.

THE FINCHES OF MAYCOMB; THE LEES OF MONROEVILLE

That garden party will go forever in *To Kill a Mockingbird*'s Maycomb, where Mrs. Dubose's camellias are in bloom, Miss Maudie's mimosas are as fragrant as ever, and wisteria drips all over the porch. Children roam freely, dewberry tarts are served, and aprons are starched. Confederate pistols are hidden, schools and churches are segregated, and Sundays are for visiting. The fictional Maycomb bears more than a passing resemblance to the landscape of the town where the novelist grew up during the Depression. "Monroevillians who read the book will see familiar names. Some events and situations are tinged with local color," said an editorial in the *Monroe Journal* in June 1960.

Monroeville is set on a square with a courthouse in the middle. That is where Harper Lee has said that she, as Scout did in the novel, spent time in the balcony watching her own lawyer father, Amasa Coleman Lee (often called A.C.) at work. "Few people live to be 80 years old and then have their name changed,"

Harper Lee poses for Life *magazine in the balcony of the old courthouse in Monroeville, Alabama, May 1961.*

the *Journal* reported, "that is what has happened to a prominent Monroeville attorney. A. C. Lee is now being called Atticus Finch." Finch was the maiden name of A.C.'s wife and Harper Lee's mother, Frances.

In 1961, when she was photographed in the balcony of the Monroe County Courthouse by *Life*, Lee told the magazine, "The trial was a composite of all the trials in the world—some in the South. But the courthouse was this one. My father was a lawyer, so I grew up in this room and mostly watched him from here. My father is one of the few men I've known with genuine humility, and it lends him a natural dignity. He has absolutely no ego drive, and so he was one of the most beloved men in this part of the state."

While Nelle Harper Lee was growing up, her lawyer father also was a state legislator (1926–1938) and the editor of the *Monroe Journal* (1929–1947). This was the Deep South, where cotton was plentiful and sharecropping the norm. Monroeville was a farming community, hard-hit during the Depression. The Hoover carts of Maycomb—mules or oxen hitched to a car because gasoline was unaffordable—were on the real-life streets of Monroeville.

The *Monroe Journal* of the thirties includes reports of a black man accused of raping a white woman, rabid-dog warnings, and ads for V. J. Elmore's, the variety store where Jem buys Scout her sequined baton in the novel. Monroeville residents remember a boy who lived in a ramshackle house near the school who was not allowed out after a run-in with the law and a schoolyard rumor that the pecans from the trees at that house were poisoned, as was said of Boo Radley's house. And a girl dressed up as a ham for an agricultural pageant as Scout did for the Halloween play.

Connecting real people, places, and events to those in the novel is a favorite pastime for residents. It fuels tourism. The old courthouse where A. C. Lee once worked is now the Monroe County Heritage Museum, a monument to *To Kill a Mockingbird* and the town it comes from. One room is set aside for Truman Capote, the author of *Breakfast at Tiffany's* and *In Cold Blood*, who was raised mainly in Monroeville by his mother's relatives until he was nine. In a display case is Capote's baby blanket and a colorful coat worn by an aunt. The museum gets twenty thousand visitors a year, says its director, Jane Ellen Clark. "We just try to answer their questions about the book, and about the town. Because everybody wants to know what was real and what wasn't. Everything that I see or hear in the book I can relate to some-

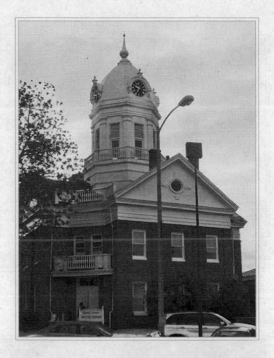

The former courthouse, now the Monroe County Heritage Museum.

thing [in Monroeville]. I do think that she was talking about her town, and her family, and all the people that she knew here."

MISS ALICE REMEMBERS

The novelist's older sister Alice Finch Lee sees it differently. "Nelle Harper says that everybody around Monroeville was determined to see themselves in the book. They would come up to her and say, 'I'm so and so in the book.' But we learned that wherever they were, they placed the book setting where they

Amasa Coleman Lee, Harper Lee's father.

Frances Finch Lee, Harper Lee's mother.

lived. Early on, Nelle Harper got a letter from a young woman in Chicago who was a doctor, and she said, 'I'm interested to know when you spent so much time in Greensboro.' Now, the only time Nelle Harper ever been to Greensboro was when she passed through it to go to school."

At the age of ninety-eight, Alice Finch Lee can still be found at her desk every day at Barnett, Bugg and Lee, the Monroeville law firm where her father worked. Alice Lee handles real estate transfers and titles when not politely declining interview requests of her sister or sorting through the boxes of fan mail.

"Everyone tries to make it an autobiography or a biography or a true story," she said to me a bit wearily. Unlike the fictional Finches, "we had a mother, we loved both parents." Frances Finch Lee, a talented musician, lived until 1951. Nelle Harper was twenty-five and Alice forty when she died.

Alice Lee described her sister as a tomboy and a gifted storyteller who had a vivid imagination all her life. "At home we were pretty much allowed to go in the direction we wanted to go, unless we were headed the wrong way. But we knew we were expected to go to Sunday school and church on Sunday, which we did. We knew we had to go to school through the week. But we were pretty much left on our resources for entertainment. Nelle Harper was very athletic. She liked to play with the little boys more than the little girls because she liked to play ball."

NELLE AND TRUMAN; SCOUT AND DILL

One of those little boys lived next door to the Lees: Truman Streckfus Persons, who later took his stepfather's name and became Truman Capote. In the novel, Dill Harris lives with his aunt Rachel next door to the Finches; he is the only character that Harper Lee has acknowledged had a model from real life. Capote based Idabel Tompkins, a character in *Other Voices, Other Rooms* (1948) on Lee. In Capote's novel, Idabel says, "Hell, I've fooled around with nobody but boys since first grade. I never think like I'm a girl, you've got to remember that or we can never be friends." That these childhood playmates from a tiny town, who once shared a beat-up old Underwood typewriter Mr. Lee

Young Truman Capote with his aunt in Monroeville, Alabama.

brought home from the newspaper, would go on to write American classics both captures and boggles the imagination.

In 1959, when *To Kill a Mockingbird* was finished but not yet published, Lee went to Holcomb, Kansas, to work on what Capote called his nonfiction novel, about the murder of a farm family. Those reporting trips became the subject of two movies *Capote* (2005) and *Infamous* (2006), and twined the two together in popular culture. By the time the movies about him appeared, Capote had been dead for more than twenty years. Lee was nearly eighty.

The childhood friendship would not survive. According to Alice Lee, Capote's envy over *To Kill a Mockingbird* winning the Pulitzer Prize consumed him. "Truman became very jealous because Nelle Harper got a Pulitzer and he did not. He expected *In Cold Blood* to bring him one, and he got involved with the drugs and heavy drinking and all. And that was it. It was not Nelle Harper dropping him. It was Truman going away from her."

In time, a persistent and untraceable rumor developed, largely fueled by the fact that Lee did not publish a second book, which suggested Capote had something to do with the writing of *To Kill a Mockingbird*. Many of the writers I interviewed rejected this notion based on style alone. Mark Childress said, "I got a letter from Harper Lee one time that absolutely proved to me that she wrote every word of *To Kill a Mockingbird* 'cause the voice is completely the voice of the book. It's the most beautifully, eloquently written letter. So I know that people are lying when they say that."

Anna Quindlan said, "Truman Capote would have ginned up all kinds of scenes in that book. You know, just by reading *To Kill a Mockingbird*, that Harper Lee, who is obviously Scout, is a person with a grounded self-esteem, surrounded by affection. Whereas you have that horrible moment where her hideous second cousin Francis, the one that she beats up and calls a whore lady with no idea what that means, says something terrible about Dill, who is based on the boy Truman Capote. He says, '[Dill] doesn't come to visit you in the summer. His mother doesn't want him and she passes him around from person to person' and you think, *oh that little boy is going to be in real trouble* and, of course, that little boy was."

WHEN A THING LIKE THIS HAPPENS TO A COUNTRY GIRL GOING TO NEW YORK

"It was somewhat of a surprise and it's very rare indeed when a thing like this happens to a country girl going to New York," A. C. Lee told his local paper in 1960.

Very rare indeed. Nelle Harper left the University of Alabama in 1948, one semester short of completing her law studies, and moved to New York to pursue writing. She supported herself as an airline ticket agent until friends, Michael and Joy Brown, gave her an unusual present on Christmas Day, 1956: the money to quit her job and write full-time for one year. "Their 'faith in me' was really all I heard them say," Lee wrote later, in a 1964 essay for *McCall's* magazine. "I would do my best not to fail them."

And so she did. By June 1957, Nelle Harper Lee had an agent and a manuscript, titled "Atticus," that was submitted to the publisher J. B. Lippincott Company. "There were many things wrong about it," editor Tay Hohoff later recalled. "It was more of a collection of short stories than a true novel. And—and yet, there was also life. It was real. The people walked solidly onto the pages; they could be seen and felt. . . . Obviously a keen and witty and even wise mind was at work; but was it the mind of

a professional novelist? There were dangling threads of a plot, there was a lack of unity—a beginning, a middle, and an end— that was inherent in the beginning. It is an indication of how seriously we were impressed by the author that we signed a contract at that point." Hohoff described the prepublication life of the novel in "We Get a New Author," an essay for the Literary Guild's magazine to promote the selection of *To Kill a Mockingbird* as its book of the month.

After the book contract was signed, two more years of work followed—"a long and hopeless period of writing the book over and over again" is how Lee described it to the *New York Times* in 1961—though there is no record to be found of the edits that were made to the manuscript. The Christmas gift from her good friends and a small advance from her publisher could only stretch so far. "It's no secret," Hohoff wrote in 1967, "that she was living on next to nothing and in considerable physical discomfort while she was writing *Mockingbird*. I don't think anyone, certainly not I, ever heard one small mutter of discontent throughout all those months of writing and tearing up, writing and tearing up."

The end result was a triumph. Even before its official publication date, *To Kill a Mockingbird* had begun to soar. It was chosen for the Literary Guild and to be condensed for the Reader's Digest Book Club. "Harper Lee's first novel sets the whole book world on fire! The reason: It makes you so glad to be alive," blared the publisher's ad for the $3.95 hardcover. "Weeks before publication the book world was talking about *To Kill a Mockingbird*. The grapevine began humming with excitement. Booksellers heard it and increased their advance orders."

SUMMER OF '60

To Kill a Mockingbird was published on July 11, 1960. It was the summer the birth-control pill was released, Elvis Presley returned to civilian life and recorded "It's Now or Never," some seven hundred U.S. military advisers were in South Vietnam, *Psycho* was in movie theaters, *Gunsmoke* was on TV, the Kennedy-Nixon campaign was just beginning, Wilma Rudolph won three gold medals at the summer Olympics in Rome, and Alan Drury's *Advise and Consent*, a novel about a secretary-of-state nominee who once had ties to the Communist Party, was at the top of the best-selling fiction list. *Better Homes and Gardens First Aid for Your Family* was moving quickly to the top of the nonfiction list.

That summer, most forms of racial segregation were not yet against the law, and civil disobedience, such as sit-ins at lunch counters, had only just begun. "People forget how divided this country was," Scott Turow said, "what the animosity was to the Civil Rights Act, which probably never would have been passed if John F. Kennedy hadn't been assassinated, and it became his legacy. But that was 1963. In 1960 there were no laws guaranteeing that African Americans could enter any restaurant, any hotel. We didn't have those laws. In that world, [for Harper Lee] to speak out this way was remarkable."

In Alabama only sixty-six thousand of the state's nearly one million blacks were registered to vote. Three years later, in his 1963 inauguration speech, Governor George Wallace vowed, "Segregation now, segregation tomorrow, and segregation forever." Six months after his inauguration, Wallace stood in the schoolhouse door refusing to integrate the University of Alabama.

In Birmingham, where the 1963 bombing of the Sixteenth Street Baptist Church that killed four young girls would become a turning point in the civil rights movement, Andrew Young was working on the Southern Christian Leadership Conference's campaign to desegregate the downtown businesses. "You had, for the first time, black people making union wages in the steel mills," he remembered. "And they began to build nice homes. These were veterans of service in the military who came back, went to school, got good jobs, and started building nice little homes, nothing fancy, just little three-bedroom frame houses. There were more than sixty of those houses dynamited [by whites in the late fifties]. *To Kill a Mockingbird* gave us the background to that, but it also gave us hope that justice could prevail. I think that's one of the things that makes it a great story, because it can be repeated in many different ways."

Childress recalled the story of how Abraham Lincoln greeted Harriet Beecher Stowe, the author of *Uncle Tom's Cabin*, in 1862. President Lincoln reportedly said, "So this is the little lady who started our big war." Childress said, "I think the same can be said of Harper Lee. This was one of the most influential novels, not necessarily in a literary sense, but in a social sense. It gives white Southerners a way to understand the racism that they've been brought up with and to find another way. And for white Southerners at that time, there was no other way. And most white people in the South were good people. Most white people in the South were not throwing bombs and causing havoc. But they had been raised in the system, and I think the book really helped them come to understand what was wrong with the system in the way that any number of treatises could never do, because it was popular art, because it was told from a child's point of view."

Rick Bragg saw the novel's impact on whites, on "young men who grew up on the wrong side of the issue that dominates this book. They start reading it, and the next thing you know, it's not just held their interest, it's changed their views. That's almost impossible. But it happens."

One of the reasons it can happen, McWhorter suggested, is that "even though *To Kill a Mockingbird* is such a classic indictment of racism, it's not really an indictment of the racist, because there's this recognition that those attitudes were 'normal' then. For someone to rebel and stand up against them was exceptional, and Atticus doesn't take that much pride in doing so, just as he would have preferred not to have to be the one to shoot the mad dog. He simply does what he must do and doesn't make a big deal about it."

HOLLYWOOD

"The big danger in making a movie of *To Kill a Mockingbird*," its director, Robert Mulligan, said to the *New York Times* in 1961, "is in thinking of this as a chance to jump on a segregation-integration soapbox. This book does not make speeches. It is not melodramatic, with race riots and race hatred. It deals with bigotry, lack of understanding, and rigid social patterns of a small Southern town." Mulligan and producer Alan Pakula first approached Harper Lee to write the screenplay. She declined, wanting to work instead on her next book. Texas playwright Horton Foote wrote what many consider to be one of the greatest screen adaptations of all time. The script, faithful to the novel, condensed the time period from three years to one, deleted many characters, and focused heavily on the mystery of Boo Radley and the trial of Tom Robinson.

"Horton Foote was the perfect person to adapt Harper Lee's book," said theatrical agent Boaty Boatwright, who cast the children in the movie. "He was a poet and he understood those people and he wrote so beautifully. She and Horton became the closest and the best of friends and stayed completely in touch until [Foote died in 2009]. There are many great books that don't make great films. And sometimes there are rather bad books that make good films. But this was a real combination. Harper loved what he did; we all did."

To Kill a Mockingbird, starring Gregory Peck as Atticus Finch and featuring Robert Duvall's wordless screen debut as Boo Radley, was released on Christmas Day, 1962. The opening credit sequence—with Steven Frankfurt's design of marbles, toys, and crayon drawings and composer Elmer Bernstein's plaintive piano notes, just the way a child would play them—stands alone.

Young Mary Badham makes a perfect Scout entrance swinging into frame on a Tarzan rope tied to a tree and dropping down. The casting was "pure genius," wrote Leo Sullivan in the *Washington Post*, calling the film "an unforgettable beautiful experience." Bosley Crowther in the *New York Times* also noted the "superb discoveries" of Badham and Phillip Alford, who played Jem.

"I know authors are supposed to knock Hollywood and complain about how their works are treated," Harper Lee told Bob Thomas of the Associated Press, "but I just can't manage it."

In Birmingham, McWhorter was in the fifth grade at the private, all-white Brooke Hill School for Girls with Mary Badham, who, at age nine, with no acting experience, got the part of Scout in the movie. The entire class watched it together. "Every Southern child has an episode of cognitive dissonance having to do with race, and it's when the beliefs that you held are suddenly contradicted. For me, it was seeing that movie. I remember watching it, first assuming that Atticus was going to get Tom Robinson off because Tom Robinson was innocent, and Atticus was played by Gregory Peck, and of course he's going to win. Then, as it dawned on me that it wasn't going to happen, I started getting upset about that. Then I started getting really upset about being upset. By rooting for a black man,

Mary Badham as Scout in the film of To Kill a Mockingbird.

you are kind of betraying every principle that you had been raised to believe. And I remember thinking, *What would my father think, if he saw me fighting back these tears when Tom Robinson gets shot?* It was a really disturbing experience. Crying tears for a black man was so taboo."

The movie amplified the novel's importance, and the two—a masterpiece in each medium—are anomalies together.

To Kill a Mockingbird received eight Academy Award nominations and forty-eight years later has the same staying power as the novel. In the last twenty years, the film has appeared on various American Film Institute lists: It was number two on the Best American Films of All Time list of 2006 (*It's a Wonderful Life* was number one), and Atticus Finch was the number one Greatest Movie Hero of the 20th Century in 2003.

"You don't get a chance to have a film and a book that makes that kind of impact," said Badham, who made two more movies and retired from acting at fourteen. "This is not a black-and-white 1930s issue. Racism and bigotry haven't gone anywhere, ignorance hasn't gone anywhere."

"A REMINDER TO THE PEOPLE AT HOME"

By March 1963, when Harper Lee turned up in Chicago to give a press conference about the film, the civil rights movement had entered the national consciousness. Times had clearly changed, as evidenced by the questions the young novelist was asked. *Rogue*, a men's magazine along the lines of *Playboy* and *Esquire*, covered the press conference. "What follows is an account of the flood of questions the noted writer must endure, all in the name of publicity," read the story, which added character descriptions and stage directions to go with dialogue.

"Harper Lee arrived. She is 36-years-old, tall, and a few pounds on the wrong side of Metrecal [a popular diet drink]. She has dark, short-cut, uncurled hair; bright, twinkling eyes; a gracious manner; and Mint Julep diction."

REPORTER: *Have you seen the movie?*

MISS LEE: *Yes. Six times. (It was soon learned that she feels the film did justice to the book, and though she did not have script approval, she enjoyed the celluloid treatment with "unbridled pleasure.")*

REPORTER: *What's going to happen when it's shown in the South?*

MISS LEE: *I don't know. But I wondered the same thing when the book was published. But the publisher said not to worry, because no one can read down there.*

PR MAN: *It opened in Florida—*

MISS LEE: *Phil, honey—that's not the South.*

REPORTER: *When you wrote the book, did you hold yourself back?*

MISS LEE *(patiently)*: *Well, sir, in the book I tried to give a sense of proportion to life in the South, that there isn't a lynching before every breakfast. I think that Southerners react with the same kind of horror as other people do about the injustice in their land. In Mississippi, people were so revolted by what happened, they were so stunned, I don't think it will happen again.*

REPORTER: *What do you think of the Freedom Riders [the civil rights activists who rode buses into the segregated South to challenge the law]?*

MISS LEE: *I don't think much of this business of getting on buses and flaunting [sic] state laws does much of anything. Except getting a lot of publicity and violence. I think Reverend King and the NAACP are going about it exactly the right way. The people in the South may not like it but they respect it.*

REPORTER *(cub variety)*: *I came in late so maybe you've already been asked this question, but I'd like to know if your book is an indictment against a group in society.*

MISS LEE *(nonplussed)*: *The book is not an indictment so much as a plea for something, a reminder to people at home.*

The people at home may not have been Lee's best audience, initially. As Rick Bragg said, "I think it was one of those books where the people down the road might shoot you a dirty look or say mean things about you as the car rolls by, but people a thousand miles away love you and admire you and think that you've done something decent and grand."

Monroeville was segregated; its public schools did not integrate until 1970—ten years after the novel was published. Mary Tucker, a teacher, said she was one of the few black residents who read the novel in 1960. White people in town, she recalled, "resented Atticus's defending a black man."

Another response was a bit of a shrug: The setting was so familiar. It was not until Gregory Peck came calling, said Jane Ellen Clark, director of the Monroe County Heritage Museum, that the town sat up and took notice. "Everybody has a story of Gregory Peck being here in this town, staying at the hotel, eating in the restaurants, and visiting Mister Lee. That's when people noticed the book. If Hollywood's gonna make a movie out of this book, then there's something about it that's special."

"THE LAY OF THE LAND THAT FORMED YOU"

Today in Monroeville a piece of the stone wall that once separated the houses of the Lees and Capote's relatives is all that's left of the old neighborhood. In the fifties, the Lee family house on South Alabama Avenue was torn down and replaced by Mel's Dairy Dream, a white shack where hot dogs and ice cream are served through a window. The spot where Capote's family once lived is now an empty lot, save for two of his aunt's camellia bushes and the remnants of a stone fishpond. There's a plaque. The streets are wider and paved, and businesses have sprawled out far beyond the town square.

Every year at the museum, the local Mockingbird Players perform a stage version of the story to raise funds for the building's maintenance. The second act takes place inside the old courtroom, and twelve ticket holders are seated as the jury. There's a gift shop with books, postcards, coffee mugs, and souvenirs such as necklaces with miniaturized movie stills of Badham, the actress who played Scout. *Mockingbird* pilgrims come and go and stop for coffee at the Bee Hive or Radley's Grille, the best restaurant and the only place to get a drink in an otherwise dry county.

Making those trips to Monroeville and trying to graft Harper Lee's life onto the novel is something readers love to do, but novelists such as Childress, who has set half of his books in Alabama, have less interest in the exercise. "Her life was probably something like the life in there," he said, "but it wasn't so beautifully dramatically shaped, and there wasn't one moment that pulled it all together. That's the beauty of fiction, that's what fiction can do: give shape to narrative."

Wally Lamb "came to a realization over the years that I bet is true of Harper Lee, as well. You start with who and what you know. You take a survey of the lay of that land that formed you and shaped you, and then you begin to lie about it. You tell one lie that turns into a different lie, and after a while those models sort of lift off and become their own people rather than the people you originally thought of. And when you weave an entire network of lies, what you're really doing, if you're aiming to write literary fiction, is, by telling lies, you're trying to arrive at a deeper truth."

James McBride said the deeper truth is all that matters. "*To Kill a Mockingbird* is rooted in reality, and it worked," he said. "When the writer gets to the mainland, nobody asks how they got there. . . . Who cares if you got there on the *Titanic*, or you paddled with a boat, or you jumped from lily pad to lily pad? You got to the mainland, and that's what counts."

"I DIDN'T EXPECT THE BOOK TO SELL IN THE FIRST PLACE"

"What was your reaction to the novel's enormous success?" radio interviewer Roy Newquist asked Harper Lee in March 1964.

"Well, I can't say it was one of surprise. It was one of sheer numbness. It was like being hit over the head and knocked out cold. You see, I never expected any sort of success with *Mockingbird*. I didn't expect the book to sell in the first place. I was hoping for a quick and merciful death at the hands of reviewers, but at the same time I sort of hoped that maybe someone would like it enough to give me encouragement. Public encouragement. I hoped for a little, as I said, but I got rather a whole lot, and in some ways this was just about as frightening as the quick merciful death I'd expected."

And that was last time Harper Lee sat for a full interview. "She did not think that a writer needed to be recognized in person and it bothered her when she got too familiar," Miss Alice explained. "As time went on she said that reporters began to take too many liberties with what she said. So, she just wanted out. And she started that and did not break her rule. She felt like she'd given enough."

But in 1966, the *Delta Review*, a New Orleans magazine, published "An Afternoon with Harper Lee," by Don Lee Keith, a curious first-person account of meeting the novelist in Monroeville. Long on description, short on quotes, it said that Lee had stopped granting personal interviews. Lee's quotations bear a striking resemblance to those in *McCalls* and *Life,* published in 1961. A former feature writer for the *New Orleans Times-Picayune*, Don Lee Keith taught journalism at the University of New Orleans until he died in 2003. His papers reside there. And while the collection has boxes filled with research, interviews, and notes on Truman Capote and Tennessee Williams, among others, there's no documentation of what went into his article about Harper Lee.

In a remembrance, former student Perry Kasprazk wrote that Keith talked about how he got that story. "Keith was fond of saying that a telephone book was a reporter's best friend. He qualified this maxim with the story of how he got one of the only eight interviews with Nelle Harper Lee. Keith called the residence of her sister, whose number he found in the telephone directory, and Harper Lee herself answered. Keith said, 'Hi, my name is Don Lee Keith, and you don't know me, but you ought to.' Charmed, she invited him over for tea and an interview."

We don't know whether Harper Lee considered that an interview or not, or what she thought about anything, really, after that. We do know her novel kept growing in stature and popularity—and shows no signs of slowing down.

"*To Kill a Mockingbird* tells a tale that we know is still true," Scott Turow said. "We may live, eventually, in a world where that kind of race prejudice is unimaginable. And people may read this story in three hundred years and say, 'So what was the big deal?' But the fact of the matter is, in today's America, it still speaks a fundamental truth."

"One of the unacknowledged powers of the novel," Gurganus said, "is that, here in this little town, in these two hundred pages, a life is saved, something is salvaged, perfect justice is achieved, however improbably. And I think that that's one of the reasons we read, is to have our faith in the process renewed."

After *To Kill a Mockingbird*, Harper Lee published four essays but not another novel, a fact that prompts speculation, lots of it. Other writers are especially good at that.

Scott Turow said, "It's a frightening thing to another novelist to write a book that good and then shut up."

Richard Russo said, "Whenever a writer is gifted enough and fortunate enough to write a book as good as that, you can't help but think, *What else?*"

David Kipen said, "I wish I could be one of these people who say, 'It's churlish to want more from a woman who's already given us so much,' but I'm a greedy reader, and I think a true reader has to be a greedy reader. I wanted the next book, and I will always feel cheated for not having gotten it."

Lee Smith said, "It's just astonishing to me that Harper Lee just stopped. I bet she hasn't. I bet she's sneaking around doing it. I bet she's sitting in her house like Boo Radley, writing. I hope so."

Oprah Winfrey said Harper Lee brought up Boo Radley when

they had lunch. "She said to me, 'You know the character Boo Radley?' And then she said, 'Well, if you know Boo, then you understand why I wouldn't be doing an interview, because I am really Boo.'"

Boo she may be, and dragging her "shy ways into the limelight" would be a sin, to quote Sheriff Tate from the novel. And so, there is no second book.

"She didn't put herself under the burden of writing like she did when she was doing *Mockingbird*. But she continued to write something. I think she was just working on maybe short things with an idea of incorporating them into something. She didn't talk too much about it." That's what Miss Alice said, and then quoted her sister. "She says you couldn't top what she had done. She told one of our cousins who asked her, 'I haven't anywhere to go, but down.'"

"Maybe for Harper Lee there was nothing else to play," James McBride said. "She sang the song, she played the solo, and she walked off the stage. And we're all the better for it. We're very grateful to her for the amount of love that she's given us."

"A love story, pure and simple" is how Harper Lee once described her first and only book. *To Kill a Mockingbird* is her love, her story, her labor. She holds its birthright. And we, readers all, gave it life.

Long may it live.

PART II

The Interviews

Mary Badham

Mary Badham was born in Birmingham, Alabama, in 1952. At the age of nine, she played Scout in the film version of To Kill a Mockingbird and was nominated for an Academy Award for Best Supporting Actress. (Patty Duke won that year for The Miracle Worker.)

After appearing in two more movies, Badham retired from acting at fourteen. More than forty years later, Badham was coaxed out of retirement—briefly—and appeared as Mrs. Nutbush in the film Our Very Own (2005). She is currently an art restorer in Virginia and frequently gives talks about her role in the film.

*T*here had been a general cattle call throughout the South, with theaters and actors in the area, as well as the general population, to let them know there was going to be an audition for *To Kill a Mockingbird*. My mom had to go to ask my dad, who said no. But my mom had him so wrapped. She said, "Now, Henry, what are the chances that the child will get the part anyway?"

When we went in for the audition, they gave us a copy of the script, and I read it and I loved it. My mom said that the next morning at the breakfast table I was popping out with lines already—Scout's lines. She knew that I had something. Evidently, I did.

I went to New York for a screen test, passed that, and went on to California to film it.

Frankly, I didn't read the book until after I had my daughter. That's embarrassing. But in defense of me, how many times have you seen a film and read the book and it totally alters your whole impression of the work? I had my whole life up there on the screen, and I was perfectly happy with the way it was.

When I did read the book, here were all these people that I never knew existed! People that we all have in our families, good or otherwise.

Learning more about the relationship of Boo was interesting.

I would love to have included the parts of the book that talked of our relationship with Calpurnia, for it was so close to my relationship with the ladies who raised me, Beddie Harris and Frankie McCall. Frankie McCall was our majordomo and raised six generations of Badhams. When the book covered going to church with Cal, we did that as children with Beddie and Frankie. We went to their houses, it was part of our upbringing.

Frankie knew more about what it was to be a lady than most white people. She expected and demanded the best from us.

Anyone who's lived in the South during that time period of the thirties through the sixties and even today, can totally relate to the feel of the book and the tempo, as far as the slowness and the way things are done. The outgoingness. People go to church, and if you don't go to church, they come to your house to check on you or call. If you are sick, they bring food. They take care of your garden if you are not able to.

I think Scout and I were so similar. I grew up in a house full of boys, so I really didn't relate to females at all. I didn't understand females. I didn't know anything about females other than my mother. That's different when it's your mother. I trailed around my brothers and nephews, and I wanted to be doing whatever they were doing. Of course, they didn't want me doing whatever they were doing, and they would try and get rid of me. I felt so attached to Scout. I just wish I could have been as smart as Scout was, always there with the comeback. Scout was a lot smarter then I was. She's a lot smarter then a lot of adults I know.

Being on the set was playtime. We had a blast. Phillip [Alford, who played Jem] said that we used to fight all the time. I don't re-member it, but he said we did. Bob Mulligan was one of the best directors ever. He would squat down and get eye to eye and talk to me like an adult. I don't ever remember him talking to us like children. He would just set up the scene for us. "The camera's gonna be here, you're gonna be here. We're gonna move this way. And then you do your line." How I delivered the lines was left to me. I could do them on the fly. I think it shows when you look at the footage now, it was brilliant.

I think we only got as much of the script as we needed to

know. I knew nothing about film. I knew nothing about the business. I was just a normal, stupid kid from Birmingham, Alabama. But evidently I had memorized all the lines. So somebody would hesitate on a line, and be thinking about how to deliver the line, and I would think that they were having trouble with their lines, so I would mouth it. And they'd say, "Cut. You can't do that, Mary. We can see you on film doing that. You can't mouth the lines." It was bad. Phillip got so mad at me for that. I'm sure everybody did. I just didn't know about film.

[For the scene in the porch swing with Gregory Peck when Atticus says, "Scout, do you know what a compromise is?"] I was supposed to cry, and I couldn't cry. I was having fun. I was happy. They tried everything. They took me off to the side and they said, "Did you ever lose a pet?" All this stuff. They finally resorted to blowing onion juice in my eye to try and help.

The ham was interesting. Whitey, our prop manager, made that ham and made it out of chicken wire and papier-mâché. We had these press photos to do, so I had to pretend that I was helping Whitey paint it. So we had to put the ham on, and I couldn't see out of it. Then they had to put a harness on to hold it off my body. When I went to take a step it was too tight. So it cut my shins. He had to cut the bottom of it off, and then they had to pad it up so that I could walk.

The tire scene: What you don't see was, off to the side there was this big utility truck. And evidently we had one of our disagreements that morning and the boys decided they just about had enough of me. They were just going to kill me and not have to deal with this anymore. So they took that tire and pushed it as hard as they could into that utility truck. After that, Bob Mulligan put a stunt double in the tire scene. You see me in the very beginning and you see me in the very end. But that long shot down the way, that's a stunt double.

"Hey, Boo" was a hard scene to do. For some reason I got tickled. And I couldn't do it. Or, I felt like I wanted to laugh and I had to do this thing. But it turned out OK.

The hardest scene by far was the jail scene, where we go looking for Atticus. The reason it was so hard was because it was the last day of filming. That was the last thing we shot, and I knew that I would have to say good-bye to all these people and I would never see any of them ever again. We'd been together long enough that these people were like family. So I didn't want to say good-bye. I didn't want it to end.

I have that long speech, [I wasn't doing my lines right], finally Mr. Mulligan called "Cut!" and my mom took me to the trailer and said, "I don't know what's going on with you, but you better get yourself together. Do you know what the freeway is like at five o'clock? These people have to go home." So I went out and I did the stuff: "Hey Mr. Cunningham" and "I know your son." It was just hard to do that whole thing, to know that I'd never see those people again.

[Gregory Peck] was my Atticus. He will always be Atticus. He was so wonderful. I miss him a lot. Years later, the phone would ring, and he'd be on the other [end of the] line. "What ya doing, kiddo?" He'd check on me just to see how I was doing because I lost my parents very early in my life. My mom died three weeks after I graduated high school. My dad died two years after I got married. When most people still have their parents, I didn't have anybody. It was kind of hard. I felt really cut off. So after they were gone, Atticus would call and check on me. If he was gonna be on the East Coast, he'd say, "I'll take you out to lunch." And whenever I'd be in California, I'd always go up to the house and visit. It really meant a lot to me. He was such a role model, and I always wanted him to be proud of me.

My father was very much like Atticus. We were raised with all those morals, all that grounding, all those same rules and regulations for females were in place. Little girls were expected to toe the line and learn to take care of the house and be mothers and wives, and that was about it. Atticus understood Scout. He didn't speak down to his children. After my daddy died, it was good to have the continuance of that male role model.

I had three daddies. There was Atticus, and there was my own daddy, and there was Brock Peters [who played Tom Robinson].

I didn't understand the importance of the film until much, much later. I didn't even get to see any of the film until we had the premiere. Then I got to see the whole story, and then I really kind of understood it.

When Scout's talking to Atticus when she comes home after the attack, and she says, "Well, it'd be sort of like shootin' a mockingbird, wouldn't it?"—her insight, picking up on the whole situation and showing that she really had been listening to everything her father says, taking it all in and looking at her life and saying, "Oh, so this is the way it is"—Scout has that realization of the other, of the world, of her community, and the changes. She is caught there between adulthood and childhood and lost somewhere in that questioning and knowledge.

You don't get a chance to have a film and a book that makes that kind of impact. The messages are so clear and so simple. It's about a way of life, getting along, and learning tolerance. This is not a black-and-white 1930s issue, this is a global issue. Racism and bigotry haven't gone anywhere. Ignorance hasn't gone anywhere.

Boaty Boatwright

International Creative Management (ICM) theatrical agent Alice Lee "Boaty" Boatwright grew up in Reidsville, North Carolina, in the fifties. She played an important role in the film; albeit offscreen. Boatwright cast the children.

I think I read *To Kill a Mockingbird* the day it came out. It was second only to *Gone with the Wind* for people to read who had ever lived in the South.

First of all, one had enormous identification with it, of what it's like to grow up in a small town. I grew up in a town where you went back and forth next door. Every small town had some kind of person that we thought was crazy or a character who maybe sat on a porch. I had a woman who worked in our house named Soola, and she reminded me a great deal of Calpurnia, the warmth, the love, the understanding. I lost my mother at seventeen. I also adored my father. I think the novel is about children and families and parents and understanding—basically, how people find a better way of understanding other people. It is so indigenous to one's childhood.

I thought I knew the characters. I identified a great deal with Scout. My best friend until I was nine years old was a little boy who lived across the street from us. His name was Philip. I think everybody goes back to some event or moment when they feel that they can identify not only with the story itself, but with the characters.

When I read *To Kill a Mockingbird*, I was living in New York and had just started working for Universal Pictures. I was doing publicity, but not in any executive capacity. Subsequently I heard that the book had been bought by Universal.

Then, quite by chance one night at a restaurant in New York, I met Alan Pakula [the producer of *To Kill a Mockingbird*], who was introduced to me by a mutual friend. I knew that Alan and Bob Mulligan [the director] had bought the book. I don't know if Greg [Gregory Peck] was in it at the very beginning or not.

Alan was so in love with books, as was Bob. They had such an amazing collaboration.

When we met, I immediately, as Alan said, wouldn't let go. I just said, "You can't do this film without letting me work on it. I want to cast the children." And I was very, very persistent. I think I wore him out.

Alan and Bob specifically said we didn't want professional children. We saw a lot of professional kids in New York. It was just something about them needing to be Southern. The Southern accent is not that easy to fake for a child.

And that's how my journey to the South started.

I'd never cast a movie before. I didn't know anything about how to do it. So I called all my friends who lived in the South. I think I covered about eight or nine cities. I started in Richmond and [went] to Charlotte, to Savannah, and to Atlanta.

I would rent a motel room. The kids would come with their mothers; some of them would be driven for hundreds of miles, and they all knew that this person from Universal Pictures was looking for Scout and for Jem and for Dill. I remember by the time I was finishing in Atlanta, I was exhausted and thinking that I did not ever want to talk to anybody under thirty again. So I called Alan and Bob, and I said, "You really have to get someone else. I just cannot go on. I'm getting brainwashed."

Alan made a deal with me. He said, "Go on to Birmingham and finish the meetings you have there, and then I'll meet you in New Orleans, and you can take the weekend off, and we'll have a good time. And then we'll go back wherever you want me, to go meet some of the children."

I still had three or four more cities to do. The next morning, I remember getting off a plane in Birmingham at six A.M., and my oldest and dearest friend from Reedsville, North Carolina, which is where I grew up, met me at the airport. She was now living in Birmingham, having married a man from there. And she said to me, "I think I've found the perfect Scout." I have to give her credit. Her name was Jene-Watt Bagwell. I started interviewing and Mary [Badham] walked in, and she was just adorable. She was wearing jeans and a little striped T-shirt. She had a very short gamine haircut.

I said, "Mary, you're just so cute. How old are you?" And she said, "Nine," [sounding] very Southern. I said, "Well, you look younger and smaller than nine." And I never will forget, she looked at me and she said, "Well, if you drank as much buttermilk and smoked as many corn silks as I do, you might be smaller too."

So I called Alan and I said, "I found Scout." Mary was not allowed to come and see me in the beginning because her father, who was a [former Air Force] general and very old-school Southern gentleman, forbade it. Mary's mother was his second wife. She was an English woman, and she'd always wanted to be an actress. And her claim to fame, apparently, was that she had once done Saint Joan on the BBC radio.

She had to bring Mary to meet me without letting the general know. I had to really play out my Southern heritage with the general. I said, "Please, let your daughter meet with the director." By this time, we had told him that I had met with her and I thought she would be the perfect Scout.

I did not think about Truman Capote when I was casting Dill. I didn't want to, because Truman was not as gracious as he might have been to Harper and the book. Certainly Dill is patterned after much of Truman. I know he used to visit in Monroeville in the summers. At his best, Truman could be a very unhappy, angry, needful person. I never heard Nelle say a word or mention him in any kind of negative way. But Nelle didn't do that, particularly in public.

Horton Foote was the perfect person to adapt Harper Lee's book. She and Horton became the closest and the best of friends and stayed totally, completely in touch until recently when Horton died. Horton was the most amazing writer himself. He was a poet, and he understood those people, and he wrote so beautifully.

He knew that his job was to adapt the book into a film, not to change the film from the book, which so often happens.

There are many great books that don't make great films. And sometimes there are rather bad books that make good films. But this was a real combination. Harper loved what he did; we all did.

The movie was shot on the back lot of Universal, and I went out for a couple of visits. I don't know the budget. I think it was no more than three million. It just was an amazing set. I can see those sidewalks and those streets and that house now.

The other thing that was so interesting was the opening credits, the opening of the cigar box. That was the genius of a man named Steve Frankfurt, who was a great friend of Alan's. I think they'd gone to Yale together.

I remember he and I went to [a] couple of schools and he had children draw pictures of mockingbirds, and that was the beautiful scene where it's torn apart. In the South, you always hear that line. I remember my own father always saying, "You never shoot a mockingbird, 'cause all they do is sing."

I first saw the movie in a small screening room at Universal. Bob Mulligan and Alan invited a few people who worked on it. I remember it didn't have a score and it hadn't been completely finished. Even so, you just knew that it was a jewel of a movie, that everybody had done their best.

I can still see Nelle [Harper Lee] sitting in Alan's living room, when we all used to gather and laugh and talk and drink and have a good time. Nelle worshipped her father. She was this amazing, incredibly talented, fiercely honest woman. She was wildly funny, witty, and smart. She certainly did not suffer fools lightly. And of course one kept hoping and waiting for the next novel. Sadly that never came.

To Kill a Mockingbird gave me my casting career. After that, Universal hired me to become a casting director on the East Coast. So I had the opportunity to work with some wonderful directors.

[Alan Pakula and Bob Mulligan dissolved their partnership in 1965. Pakula became a director of films, such as *Klute*, *All the President's Men*, and *Sophie's Choice*. He died in 1998. Mulligan directed eleven more films, including *Up the Down Staircase*, *Summer of '42*, and *Same Time, Next Year*. He died in 2008.]

Rick Bragg

Rick Bragg was born in Piedmont, Alabama, in 1959. He is a Pulitzer Prize—winning reporter and the author of the memoirs All Over but the Shoutin' *(1999),* Ava's Man *(2002), and* Prince of Frogtown *(2008). Bragg grew up in Trout Possum, Alabama, and was the winner of the Harper Lee Award at the Alabama Writers Symposium in 2009. He teaches at the University of Alabama.*

*L*ike a lot of people, I was in school when I read *To Kill a Mockingbird*. They were always sneaking adult books into our consciousness back then. And like a lot of people, I was told to read it. And like a lot of people, you start that way, with that kind of grudging, *Let's get this done*. And within paragraphs—you hear that over and over again, especially from young men that have been forced to read it, young men who grew up on the wrong side of the issue that dominates this book—they start reading it, and the next thing you know, it's not just held their interest, it's changed their views. That's pretty damn . . . that's almost impossible, but it happens.

I think it means a lot to Southerners. I was born in '59, grew up as a baby boy in the civil rights movement, and it was as though it was invisible. When I was six or seven, I remember scenes and incidents of violence, but for those of us in the mountains, it was as though it was invisible. And then you read this book, and you retroactively tug back into that time and that struggle, and you ask yourself, "How in the world did I miss this? How did I not know this was happening?"

There's a south Alabama feel to the book. There's a much more parochial feel to that place than where I grew up, which was predominantly white. I grew up in the mountains. There was a whole different dynamic going on there. I grew up in the industrial South. I grew up in the steel mills and pipe shops and textile mills, cotton mills. I grew up in a more hillbilly, for lack of a better word, culture than in any kind of south Alabama, agrarian culture.

I've read it twice, three times. Probably, like a lot of people, I'll read parts of it to reaffirm or recondition [myself].

The first time I read it, it was pretty cut-and-dried. It was do right or don't do right. Then you begin to see other themes, like tolerance and kindness. Boo seemed like a much smaller kind of subplot to the book the first time I read it. It was all about the court case, it was all about the attack, and it was all about the wrongdoing of sending that man to jail. But Boo took on a bigger role as I read it down the line.

The writing—it's just wonderful, and to get a six foot three, 280-pound man to say wonderful is hard enough, but Harper Lee did the thing you gotta do to make people care about something, which is to keep them in the story. And the phrases were beautiful. The descriptions were beautiful. The most clichéd, worn phrase from the whole book, when Atticus is talking to his children about the mockingbird, you know, that is beautiful.

My people never knew about the mockingbird. We knew it was a sin to kill a dove, because a dove had a biblical significance. It was a sign of hope in a world drowned for its sins in the great flood. But the feeling was the same. It was so real, it was so true to the dirt and the trees and the houses and the dusty streets and the mad dogs, and the sheriff who wants to do right if he can just figure out how, and the mean-spirited neighbor and the kind people in town, and the racial prejudice and the handful of people who just didn't fall in step. All that, it wasn't just true; it was beautifully, beautifully done.

I don't even think I can get my head around whether it's literature or not. I'm probably not smart enough to have that discussion. I think pretensions kill and smudge more good writing than just about anything else. I would have loved for there to have been one more book, and that's the most I can say—[but] we have that wonderful cliché, "Go out with a win."

I have been told that Harper Lee liked my work, she liked my writing. She and my wife have exchanged notes. I never wanted to be—and I don't care if this sounds bad—I never wanted to be one of those Southern writers sucking up to this legendary figure. If she wanted her privacy, then I should give it to her. So I was never one of those people. I'm like everybody else down in my part of the world—I feel like I know her. You hear things she says. You hear, "Well, she likes to be called Nelle." Before you know it, you're thinking about her as Nelle. And then there's just the book, there's always the book. If you want to know what's in her heart, in her consciousness, then go open the book. The truth is, you just open that book and you just start pulling things from it that you spent a lifetime thinking about. They just get stuck in you, notions and ideas, and, for lack of a better word, these moralities get stuck in you and may not save you, may not make you do the right thing, but at least you know when you're doing the wrong thing. Sometimes down here we have to settle for that.

I think it was very brave to write it. I also think it was one of those books where the people down the road might shoot you a dirty look or say mean things about you as the car rolls by, but people a thousand miles away love you and admire you and think that you've done something decent and grand.

I finally did meet her. The spring I won the Harper Lee Award, I asked a friend of hers, the writer Wayne Greenhaw, if I could just say hello and shake her hand. My wife, Dianne, went with me. She was kind and gracious and funny, and it was one of the nicer moments of my life. I would have hated not to have done that, I believe, in my old age.

Tom Brokaw

*Tom Brokaw was born in 1940 in Webster, South Dakota. He is an
NBC News special correspondent and the author of* The Greatest
Generation *(1998),* A Long Way Home: Growing Up in
the American Heartland *(2002), and* Boom! Voices of the
Sixties *(2006).*

I was still in college when *To Kill a Mockingbird* came out in 1960. I remember it had a kind of an electrifying effect on this country; this was a time when there were a lot of good books coming out. The sixties were very ripe. We were reading a lot about race, and we were reading what they call literary fiction now. William Styron was writing, James Baldwin was writing essays, and then this book just ricocheted around the country.

I had always been interested in race and racial justice, but mostly it was with my nose pressed up against the glass, looking at the South from a long way away. Because I lived in construction towns, we had a lot of workers who came from the South. They were all white, and, sorry to say, a number of them were pretty redneck. It just didn't comport with my family's view of how Negroes should be treated. But I did have all this curiosity about it.

And when I read *To Kill a Mockingbird*, I was so struck by the universality of small towns. I had lived in small towns in South Dakota, and I knew then, reading about Atticus, not just the pressures that he was under, but the magnifying glass that he lived in—he was the upstanding legislator and lawyer but also was part of the fabric of that town—and then the complexity of the issues that came before him and the way it divided the community. All this takes place in a very small environment. People who live in big cities, I don't think, have any idea of what the pressures can be like in a small town when there's something as controversial as that going on. It's tough. So it stuck with me for a long time.

Later, of course, it was hard for me to separate the book from the movie, because you'd see the movie a lot, and then you'd remember passages and go back and look at the book again.

But it was one of those memorable pieces of literary fiction that came along at an impressionable time in my life, and also in the country's life. Dr. King had already started the movement at that point, we were paying attention on national television every night on the network news to what was going on in the South, and this book spoke to us.

I knew people like that, who were willing to stand up in these kinds of communities against the conventional wisdom of the time. Racism didn't stop at the Mason-Dixon Line. A lot of those same attitudes were in the communities where I lived, way north, on the Great Plains. And yet there were brave people, men and women, who would speak out against them, in churches, in the business community, or wherever. But for Harper Lee to be there in the epicenter, if you will, of all this, to be so eloquent in how she described it, it shows such great courage in how she describes it. She was in that pantheon, I think, of people who helped us get liberated from racism in this country. I've been doing some work on the anniversary of Dr. King's death, and one of the most telling lines that I hear from early pioneers in the movement is: "We had liberated not just black people, we liberated white people." I think that Harper Lee helped liberate white people with that book.

Scout is irresistible, she's just irresistible. And later I became the father of daughters, and I had those kinds of conversations with my own children—they had great curiosity and their kind of tomboy attitudes, and they were tough on me. They would come to me, just like Scout did. "Why are you doing this? Have you thought this through?" I think that they could identify with her. I still have letters that my daughters wrote to me about things that I thought they should do, and they had their own minds made up about why they were going to do it. And they were good lawyer's briefs. I like to think that as Scout grew older, that she would have evolved in the same way as a teenager. We hear her voice, obviously. I think there is a really distinct relationship between fathers and daughters, and one of the things that happens, if there's a mother around, is that when the girls get to be around thirteen, they go to war with their mothers, and then the fathers are sanctuaries in some ways or the intermediaries.

So Scout will always be in my mind when I think about this book, about the whole idea of this little towheaded kid running around, sitting up in the balcony of the courthouse with the Negroes as they watch the trial unfold, questioning her father about why he was representing the defendant in this case, and the kind of taunting that she received at school.

What I thought, when I went back and read those passages again, there was this absence of piety, which I think makes the book really honest. There was self-doubt. Atticus knew that he wasn't a perfect man. He tried as best he could to give Scout the big context of what he was doing and why he was doing it. In her youthful innocence, she was asking all the right questions. So it's no wonder to me why it's so popular as a book and it will be for a long time.

I was particularly taken with when Scout went to him after she'd been taunted at school that her daddy was just nothing but an n-lover, and she asked him why he was doing this, and I still have the same reaction: I think, *Oh well, oh, now here it comes, because this is what I must do.* And it wasn't that. It was more complicated than that. You can see him working his way through why he was going to take this case, and he couldn't hold his head up unless he took this case. And he knew that there would be consequences for him, and that conversation, the dialogue between the two of them, is sophisticated in its own way, and yet it's still between a father and a daughter. I've always loved that, for all those reasons: the personal relationships, the meaning of being a lawyer, what it's like to be in a small town. Then, of course, when you have a black defendant wrongly accused in the 1930s in the white South, there was no more explosive issue than that one.

Another one of my very favorite passages in the book is a small one, but I've always loved the literary construct of it. We have the mysterious figure, Boo, who's living next door. And then of course there's the climactic episode: Jem is in bed, he's been hurt, beaten up. What's going to happen to him? And Scout goes in to see her brother. And there standing in the shadows is this mysterious neighbor. And she turns and says, "Hey, Boo." I just love that moment. It's such a personal connection, and she's absolutely unafraid of him, which is what I love. And again, to go back to the small-town culture, every town has a Boo. People don't know how to approach Boo in those small towns, in most instances. Scout did. I have used that phrase countless times in my own life; when I want to get someone's attention, I'll say, "Hey, Boo."

The Reverend Thomas Lane Butts

The Reverend Thomas Lane Butts was born in Bermuda, Alabama, in 1930. He is the pastor emeritus of the First Methodist Church in Monroeville, Alabama, attended by the Lee family. He is the author of Tigers in the Dark *(1994), a collection of his sermons.*

I was in Mobile as a pastor of the Michigan Avenue Methodist Church. I had gone through an encounter with the Ku Klux Klan. They were after me because I'd signed a petition to integrate the buses there. This was in 1960 when *To Kill a Mockingbird* came out, and it was a great comfort to those of us who had taken some stand on this particular issue.

The book was written in a way that it could not be refuted. It was a soft opposition to people who were against civil rights. It was just a great comfort to those of us who had been involved in the civil rights movement that somebody from the Deep South had given us a book that gave some comfort to us in what we had done. That was my first encounter with *To Kill a Mockingbird*.

It was great encouragement—and still is great encouragement to anybody who's involved in the civil rights movement. It made a tremendous difference in the civil rights movement, and it continues to make a difference. You would think that a novel would play out after a while. There are still civil rights issues, and the concept in this book is large enough to include other civil rights causes. It's still read with interest because of that. Plus, it's a real interesting story, wonderfully told, with a lot of good humor in it, along with the serious moments. It is obviously a well-loved book, not only in this country but around the world.

There are aspects of the book that were interesting to me that were not a part of the central drama. For instance, in that book you can see where a child learns values: at home. And you don't worry so much anymore about children not listening to you. You worry because they're watching you.

Here a single parent bringing up children is able to instill values in them that are far ahead of their time. This is one of my favorite aspects of the book.

Harper Lee refers to it as a love story. And she said, "I don't mean romantic love, but it is a love story." How love flows beyond the boundaries of affection for one person or even one family, but caring for everybody. It's love in its finest understanding of the meaning of the word.

Harper Lee developed her characters in such a marvelous way. Naturally, everybody would identify with Atticus; I like that character. But I like the sheriff. The sheriff was caught in between the people who voted for him and the issue at hand. And he handled it wonderfully well, with great thoughtfulness. When he came to the part about Boo Radley having killed a man, his decision about what to do about that was overriding what Atticus thought should be done. And he said, "You know, I may not be much, but I am the sheriff." So I liked that part too.

The book is not supposed to be autobiographical, but all novels have some autobiography in them, and all autobiographies have some fiction in them too.

I was born and reared ten miles from where the author and her family lived. We did not know their family personally because we were in another county, but Harper Lee's older sister Alice was a mentor to me as a young minister. She was always advocating my ministry and pushing me and helping me every way that she could.

I didn't meet Harper Lee until twenty-five or thirty years ago. She was able to attend the church with great regularity when she was in town. I was her pastor for five years, and still her ministerial friend to this good day.

I understood the context in which the book was written, because that's how I grew up. It was a rural, poverty-stricken situation during the Depression, where people did not have much. It was hardscrabble for most people to make a living. It was a time in which black people were treated terribly and people took in racism with their mother's milk. Here in this novel, you have a person bucking the tradition in order to advocate the rights of a person without regard to color. But it also was the farming aspect of it, people coming to town with their mules and wagons, the streets being muddy. I remember all of that and the little towns that surrounded the rural area in which I grew up during the Great Depression.

People were provincial. They cared about one another. They were stuck with certain customs they were unwilling to give up. And in fact, in the Deep South, we've never stopped fighting the Civil War; it's still going on in the minds of some people, and it's hard to get them beyond that. But basically the people in the South are very loving and caring people. People in the South are storytellers. That's how they pass on tradition from one generation to the other, by storytelling. That's how I grew up.

Everybody suffered during the Depression. It was just a matter of degree. But the Lee household was a household that espoused values that were ahead of the times in which they lived. That was obvious. Miss Alice, ever since I can remember her, has been very much associated with the church and espousing the kind of values which she learned at home. She's one of my idols, by the way. She's a great lady.

Miss Alice is very thoughtful and slow moving, very wise in her counsel and would not take any risks. She is a good guide. Nelle Harper is a more impulsive person and more expressive of her thoughts and ideas. They're both brilliant people, but they have different temperaments. Nelle Harper tends to sparkle, whereas Alice is very quiet and reserved. Nelle Harper loves to travel and to go to the exciting places. Miss Alice would not do that, but she enjoys knowing that Nelle Harper's doing it. She vicariously enjoys the things that Nelle Harper enjoys.

Alice comes to work at age ninety-eight dressed in the kind of clothing that you might have expected a woman to be wearing in 1940. The only difference now is she wears tennis shoes with them. But they are different. They complement each other. And it has always been very interesting to me to be with both of them.

For a long time, my wife, Hilda, and I would go with Nelle Harper and Alice out to Daily's Catfish every Saturday for lunch. We'd sit in the same place, order the same thing. And the conversation that would go on between the two of them and around the table was just a wonderful enlightened conversation about the times. Both of them [are] grounded in great values. They hold on to old values, which is the tradition of this town and of this area.

I once referred to Nelle Harper as being conservative, and she corrected me. She said, "I'm not conservative. I'm independent."

Today, the Monroeville town square—it looks like the book. You walk up on the square and look at the storefronts around it and the old courthouse. You can close your eyes and imagine that you are back in the days of that book. Monroeville has changed a lot, but it still holds a lot of the traditions and understandings of reality that were extant in [the thirties]. In other ways, it is a modern town. People are very highly educated. In the church where I was the pastor, I had a very highly educated congregation.

People around here keep up with Nelle Harper, but they're also very protective of her. If an outsider comes in and tries to find where Harper Lee is, nobody will tell them. Many people who are looking for Harper Lee end up in my office, because a few stories have gotten out about my being a friend of hers, but the people in this town are protective of her. They care about her a great deal.

A lot of people think that she's a recluse, which is absolutely untrue. She's a person who enjoys her privacy like any other citizen would. She's not reclusive; it's very different from that. She's open, she loves to be around people and associate with people. She does not like to be exploited by people. And she does not like to have her works exploited for profit by people.

For instance, for many years she would come to the bookshops here in town and autograph books for them to sell. And she wanted them to be sold for the same price they would ordinarily be sold for. She quit doing that when she discovered that people started taking signed books of hers and selling them on eBay for several hundred dollars. She quit signing books because she did not want people using her signature to exploit people in any way.

She has to be careful about how she relates to people, because she will get exploited. Any person who is a famous person, a celebrity, ends up in a situation where they are exploited by people trying to get their signature, have their picture made with them, or have a little bit of the reflected glory of that person in their own life. It happens. It happens.

But she is a real good person. She'd give you the shirt off her back.

She's just a common ordinary person with a brilliant mind who knows how to put a sentence together and a paragraph in an unusual way. If you were to read letters that she's written, it's almost like a chapter in a book.

She's funny in a smart way, in a brilliant sort of way. Her humor is not crass but a classical kind of humor, describing things, and describing people and situations in which she has found herself from time to time. Her storytelling is almost like the writing of *To Kill a Mockingbird*.

She's the sort of a friend that I'd say anything to. You don't have to pretend to be somebody you're not around her simply because she's a celebrity. We argue about issues and argue about the meaning of things almost like a brother and a sister would discuss things with each other. We are very close friends.

Being famous and a celebrity is probably a lot of fun the first two or three months, but after you've been a celebrity for fifty years, I'm quite sure it gets old, when you have people look at you not for who you are but for the image that they have of you. And there are a lot of mythologies that get developed about her and about her relationship to Truman Capote. There are people who ask me, "Are you sure that Nelle Harper Lee wrote *To Kill a Mockingbird*, or did Truman Capote write it?"

Well, if you read the two authors, it's very obvious that Truman Capote did not write *To Kill a Mockingbird*. But Nelle Harper did help him write and do the research for *In Cold Blood* and went to Kansas and helped him. But there are a lot of mythologies that developed, and it's hard to disabuse people of the thought that maybe she didn't write that entire book, that maybe Truman did help her, which really isn't true.

We would like to think that she would write something else. But one book's been enough for her. It's been enough. She has controlled her own destiny. She doesn't have a PR person. She doesn't need one. The fact that she doesn't give interviews makes everybody all the more interested in her and in her life and in her book. I think she has led a happier life and certainly more contented life because she has chosen how she has related to the public. It's been with care and great caution that she's done so. She is a proud but a humble person. She loves people; she does a lot of good that nobody ever knows about. She does a lot of good through the church.

You read that book and you see how you ought to rear children; you see how you ought to relate to your fellow citizens. You see what your attitude should be toward people who are different. And that is an issue in every age.

The persons may differ, but the issues are still there. And this book addresses those issues in an interesting and gentle way. It doesn't push them on you, but you can't read the book without seeing those values.

Rosanne Cash

Rosanne Cash was born in Memphis, Tennessee, in 1955. Her fourteen albums include Seven Year Ache *(1981),* The Wheel *(1993),* Black Cadillac *(2006), and* The List *(2009). She is the author of* Bodies of Water *(1996), a short story collection;* Penelope Jane *(2000), a children's book; and* Composed *(2010), a memoir.*

I was born in Memphis. I wasn't raised in the South, but I've spent plenty of time there. It makes me proud. It's the perfect Southern story. This whole book is a guide to parenting, number one. And then the language, of course. The naturalness that Atticus has with his children—there isn't this sense of modern angst about parenting. There is a beautiful intimacy between Atticus and Scout that you just want to get inside and that gives you so much feeling of love and comfort and integrity. Its beauty never ceases to amaze me and strike me. There's just this beautiful naturalness that he has and sense of confidence in his own skill as a parent. And respect for the child, that mutual respect. I just love it so much, it just gives so much satisfaction to read it.

It's perfect. She created a whole world inside these pages that we get to enter in forever. It's perfect.

I don't remember the act of reading it for the first time, but I remember taking that feeling of integrity and sense of conscience and the idea that the way you behaved, whether people saw you or not, was central to becoming yourself, becoming who you were going to become in the world, that you had to first carve out a central sense of conscience.

My daughters have read it on their own. I'm looking forward to reading it to my son. He's not quite ready, but I think very soon. These kinds of people are rare in modern life—someone with absolute integrity. Atticus is a real grown-up. He knows who he is. He knows what's right and wrong. He acts out of compassion and personal integrity.

Those lessons you learn from your parents, the really key, profound life lessons, they're seared in your memory. They're few and they're precious, and this book makes poetry of it. If you find people like that, hold on to them; they are few and far between.

Mark Childress

Mark Childress was born in Monroeville, Alabama, in 1957, and grew up in Mississippi. He is the author of six novels, including Crazy in Alabama *(1993),* Gone for Good *(1998), and* One Mississippi *(2006).*

The first time I read *To Kill a Mockingbird* I was in Monroeville, Alabama. It was two doors down from Nelle Harper Lee's house. And I was on the porch of Miss Wanda Biggs's house. Miss Wanda Biggs was my mother's best friend. She was one of Monroeville's notable busybodies. She was the Welcome Wagon lady, who chased Gregory Peck all over town to give him a welcome basket. She also operated a switchboard from her home. She got the doctors and the lawyers, and she answered phone calls for everybody. So she knew everything that was going on in town.

I was about nine years old, and she said, "I think it's time for you to read this." She put it in my hands, and it was a first edition signed to her that I'm sure I spilled Coca-Cola on, and every other thing. God, I wish I had that book. Every few hours she would wander out and say, "Now you see that stump over there? That's the tree where Boo hid the presents for the children. Did you get to the part yet about the school? If you go down this little pathway, that is where the school is."

That was the first adult novel that I had ever read, and I was just about the age of Scout when I read it, and I was reading it in the setting where it happened. And it's the reason I'm a writer today—something about seeing that ugly little town, which at that point had been sort of stripped of all of its charms, transformed into this magical thing that was in my hands. I guess it would be like if you came from Reggie Jackson's hometown, you'd want to be a baseball player.

It became real to me that Miss Wanda knew the lady who wrote this, that this was a novel written out of this place where I was right now, and how it somehow became this magic on the page. I'll never forget being in that swing reading it. It took me about three days. I read it about every year, just as a refresher course. It's a really good book.

Every time I go back, I'm impressed more by the simplicity of the prose. I think the reason that we think it's so classic is that the prose is not adorned; it's very plain. Although it's plainly written from the point of view of an adult, looking back through a child's eyes, there's something beautifully innocent about the point of view, and yet it's very wise. So it's a combination of either a wise child or an innocent adult, the point of view.

The fact that Scout is surprised by people's racism is what was revolutionary about the book. Most little kids in little towns like that, they weren't surprised, because racism was all around them. It was the fabric of life. When I was three years old, my grandmother and I would walk down the main street of Greeneville, which was the little town where she lived, and black men would get off the sidewalk as a sign of respect. And if I walked down the sidewalk, at five years old—by myself—they would get off the sidewalk as a sign of respect to me. And this was in the mid-sixties, after the book came out.

We think of this book as being a post–civil rights novel, but it was published before the biggest explosions of the civil rights movement, and helped bring it along, I think. You know that famous quote Lincoln [reportedly] said to Harriet Beecher Stowe, "Oh, here's the little lady whose book caused such a big war." I think the same can be said of Harper Lee, that *To Kill a Mockingbird* was one of the most influential novels, not necessarily in a literary sense, but in a social sense.

It gives white Southerners a way to understand the racism that they've been brought up with and to find another way. And for white Southerners at that time, there was no other way. There were either outsiders yelling at you because you were a racist cracker, or your leaders, George Wallace saying, "I'll never be out-niggered again." There was no middle ground. Most white people in the South were good people. Most white people in the South were not throwing bombs and causing havoc, but they had been raised in the system. I think the book really helped them come to understand what was wrong with the system in a way that any number of treatises could never do, because it was popular art, told from a child's point of view.

We think of it as a contemporary book, but it is set in the thirties. So it also helped the white Southerner because there was distance between the South she was writing about and the present day when it was published. That allowed them to feel, "Well, we've moved a little beyond that." And because she was a white Southerner, there was something that allowed them to hear what she was trying to say.

It's just a child trying to understand, trying to make sense of something that doesn't make any sense, trying to organize it. I guess I've spent my whole writing career trying to do the same thing, laboring in the shadow of making sense of what race meant in the South. How do you grow up having come from that system? It's a lot of interesting problems.

I don't think that kids today read it with the same edge that we did as children, because the segregation was still very real when I was reading that book. When I went to the swimming pool, there were no colored children allowed. The signs said WHITE and COLORED. When we went to the Dairy Queen, there were two lines: There was a white window, and there was a black window. So, it was a radical book at that time in the South. It might not have been that way in the rest of the country, but it said radical things.

There are a lot of people in the novel who are not quite what they seem, and there's a few people who are what they seem, and they're the heroes of the book—Miss Maudie, and Atticus, and old Boo, too.

Scout was about half boy. Scout's a real tomboy, you know, and Dill was about half girl. The two of them, they were both odd birds in their town, which is sort of the other theme that runs through the book. They're not like the other kids either. If you notice any time that other kids are seen in the book, it's always in opposition; our little group is never playing with them. And I think there's one moment where she talks about it, because she was the daughter of the lawyer, people thought she was above them. There's some stuff about the social stratification of the town too, that is really interesting. There's just a lot in the book. And that's why I keep rereading it, because I always find something new.

I was looking at the movie recently and realizing how much Gregory Peck made the movie Atticus's movie. And the book is really Scout's book. It's Scout and Jem's book. It's really about the children's learning; the whole town teaches them a little bit at a time.

I don't really remember Dill from my first reading of the book. It's kind of that weird little kid in the movie made a bigger impression on me. So that's one of the elements of the book I find hard to separate from the movie, because I saw the movie four or five years after I read the book.

It's really well done. Scout's entrance is one of the greatest entrances in movie history. She swings into the frame on the tire swing and drops. It's just so Scout, it's perfect. And it's a beautiful script. I think probably Miss Nelle would be the first to say that Horton Foote adapted that with infinite care and it's one of those rare cases where the movie's not as good as the book but it's right up there and doesn't take away from the book.

Atticus—what can you say about him? When you were a kid, you wanted to have a dad like that. There's something a little bit idealized about him. And I'm sure that's the way with all great heroes of fiction. He's a little bit too good to be true, but in the book he's got more bumps than he's allowed to have in the movie. So I like him a little better in the book. He's more recognizable to me.

Whenever people talk to me because I was born there, they say, "What's in the water in Monroeville?" Well, there's nothing in the water, but it's like I said, the most famous person in Alabama was Harper Lee. She was a novelist. I think most kids never meet a novelist.

Miss Wanda was pointing out to me the parts of it that were physically real. I think she was doing that to keep me going through the book. She didn't realize that I was completely hooked on it. It's something that really fascinates readers, like which part's true, which part is made up. And I've never quite understood that. To me, everything in a novel's real, and I really don't care where the author got it. But for readers that is important. They love to know how much of it was autobiographical.

Any writer who says he doesn't write out of his own life is lying. Of course he does—all your writing is based on your own life. But it's "Do you transform the material?" And I think that's what she did, and put such magic on it. But yeah, her life was probably something like the life in there, but it wasn't so beautifully dramatically shaped, and there wasn't one moment that pulled it all together. That's the beauty of fiction, that's what fiction can do: give shape to narrative.

I have absolutely no idea why she never published another book. But I don't blame her, and I think in a way it was probably the right decision, although I sure would love to have had the other books. When you bat the ball out [of] the park the very first time you ever step up, why would you ever pick up the bat again? I think she was very wise to stay away from it. She's probably had a much happier life because she did that. I think, for some people, publicity's just like poison. I think she had just enough of it, just enough fame right there at the beginning that, one day, she probably woke up and said, "I don't want to do this anymore." It might also have been knowing Truman and watching what it was doing to him at that point in their lives. Even though he was wildly famous and successful, he wasn't very happy. I think she probably saw that.

It takes a kind of courage that almost nobody has in this country, where celebrity is our religion; it's replaced religion for a lot of people. To turn away from the church of publicity and say, "I'm not going to pray there. I'm not going to appear there. I don't want my picture." It's a kind of blasphemy in this society that she commits by refusing to participate in the publicity machine. I certainly understand that impulse she had, to close the door and go back to her private life.

Of course, she had the great freedom of being able to live off the proceeds of her book, which most writers don't have. So, you know, that liberated her to be able to do that. If the book had sold four thousand copies, I bet you there would have been a second novel, and I bet you she'd have been out there hustling just like the rest of us!

I hope she kept writing, because she's a beautiful writer. I used to hear those rumors Truman helped her write it, or Truman wrote it for her. There's a kind of hostility in that that always took me aback. In the first place, it's a sexist assumption that somehow she couldn't do it without his help. I think the reverse is probably truer, that he couldn't have done *In Cold Blood* [without her], because a lot of those people in Kansas wouldn't talk to him. I bet you he helped her with *To Kill a Mockingbird*. I'll bet he gave it a read. I bet he went through it with his pencil. That's what friends do for each other.

Maybe it's just because she never published another book that people assume that she had to have had some help, that she couldn't do it over again the second time. I got a letter from her one time that absolutely proved to me that she wrote every word of *To Kill a Mockingbird*, 'cause the voice is completely the voice of the book. It's the most beautifully, eloquently written letter. So I know that people are lying when they say that.

To be honest, I think she's probably enjoyed playing the recluse. She has a great sense of humor—just read the book. I think it probably gives her pleasure to watch people chase after her. I think that's probably kind of fun.

She goes out and lives her life. Luckily, even the most famous writer in America can be anonymous. I guess Truman couldn't have gone much of anywhere without being recognized. But most writers can. And I think that's probably why she's kept her hand in, staying in Monroeville. People leave her alone there. And when she lives in New York, people leave her alone. So it's a pretty good life she's got going.

I've had some friends who've had huge success with their first book and have spent the rest of their careers where every review begins with "the author of the previous book" and this one doesn't ever quite measure up. The reviews were bound to be bad in comparison to *To Kill a Mockingbird*.

I wouldn't have wanted that kind of success, though, on my

first book. No way. It would have killed my career the way it did hers. I would love to have had her as a functioning writer, writing ten novels so that I could sit down, read, and wait for the new Harper Lee novel to come out, but I think the success of the book took that away from us. I think the success was just too much, and she just didn't want to go there, she didn't want to wade into that. I don't blame her.

Jane Ellen Clark

Jane Ellen Clark was born in Pensacola, Florida, in 1948. She is the executive director of the Monroe County Heritage Museum in Monroeville, Alabama.

*T*he first time I remember reading *To Kill a Mockingbird* was in 1996, when I started working here. I got calls from teachers who wanted to know things about the book that were real. They would call and ask about a character. The first question I got that I didn't know the answer to was, "Who in the town was Mister Avery?" I didn't even know who Mister Avery was. So I had to quickly get the book and look that up. He's the boarder at Miss Maudie's.

What I discovered that year was how multilayered this book is. And now, I like to listen to it. I really hear things when it's being read to me. Many of the teachers who come here tell me that they read this book aloud to their students every year—the whole book—because they love to read it.

As I learn more about Monroe County history, I hear things in the book that I relate to something. I think the last thing was Barker's Eddy in the book. I thought that's an interesting way to describe the creek. 'Cause I know what an eddy is in a river. So I thought, *Hmm, in a creek, would that be the same thing?*

So I started asking around, and just by accident found out that all the kids in Monroeville in the thirties and forties went to a Parker's Eddy to learn to swim. I said, "Why do you call it an eddy?" It's a creek that is really close to the Alabama River and when the river's high, the water does come back in. So that's why they call it an eddy. The people I asked would say "Gosh, I need to go back down there and see if that's still a good swimming hole."

Everything that I see or hear in the book I can relate to something. There's a passage about the chapel at Finch's Landing, the organ in the chapel. I live up in the north part of the county in Old Bell's Landing, and our little Methodist church has a pump organ. We grew up singing hymns as my aunt played the pump organ.

I think the town in the book is really close to the town of Monroeville in the thirties. I do also hear, though, from people all over the country who say, "It's a lot like my little town." I love to hear that, because it makes me feel good that there are towns like that out there, that we're not the only one. We have a lot of history here, and we care about it, so I'm glad that there are other people who relate to it like I do. But I do think that she was talking about her town, and her family, and all the people that she knew here, situations here. George Thomas Jones [a town historian] said to me the other day, "Well, you know, we were here. We knew all those people, all those situations that she's writing about. But could we write a Pulitzer Prize–winning book about it that has never been out of print? No. That's her genius."

My mother was in the same room at school with Harper Lee. I grew up coming here from Pensacola, up to the family land. We'd go right by the school, the site of the house of the recluse that becomes Boo Radley [in the book], that's the neighborhood of Monroeville that I think Harper Lee made into Maycomb. Mama would say things as we would come by. She told about Son Boulware, who was the boy who was put into the house, and how scared they were of him, how spooky the house was. Some people in town remember the incident. [After Son Boulware was caught breaking into a store,] his father took him home and said, "My son won't go to reform school." Some say that the boys in his class would go visit and he would help them with their algebra. But the next year, he didn't come back to school, and then those boys left. By the time my mother was ten, around 1936, nobody had seen him. All the legends had built up, and by then the kids were scared to even ride their bikes by the front of the house. I went to the cemetery to try to find his grave and found out his full name. It's Alfred Boulware. The epitaph is so wonderful: "To live in hearts left behind is not to die." [Boo] really is the hero in the end. He saves the children's life. So Harper Lee saw something else about that boy that my mother and the rest of the kids didn't.

Mama was a country kid who had to ride the bus in, and the buses weren't like we have now. They were trucks with benches in the back—covered, though. She would have to come to town with her lunch, or with a nickel to go across the street, 'cause there was a little store across from the elementary school to get something to eat.

She always told me when we passed that schoolyard, "Oh, yes, one day we were out there playing, and you weren't supposed to slide into base. I was on first base, and Nelle Harper slid in and knocked me down in that red clay, and she knew I couldn't go home at lunch to change." So fifty years later, Mama still remembers being embarrassed with the red clay stains on her clothes.

People in town say that Mister A. C. Lee, Harper Lee's father, was a lot like the character of Atticus—soft-spoken, dignified, and did the right thing. The only character Harper Lee says is real is Dill, who was Truman Capote. People in town say the same thing.

Monroeville in the 1930s was very much like the [town in] the book. Just the other day, Ann Farish, who grew up here and was in the same room at school with Harper Lee, said to me that she and her friend would go down the alleys off the stores here on the square to look for change. She said, "You know, men had holes in their pockets. Times were hard. We wore our clothes until they had holes in 'em." So the things that I read in this book, I'm also finding in interviews with people, and things that have been written about the time.

They say that [Monroeville in the thirties] was only about one or two blocks out from the square. The square was the center of town. And Saturday was the shopping day, when all the country people would come to town. Even in the sixties, I remember coming through Monroeville, and there would be people that came to town to shop with their wagon and mules. So when she talks about the Hoover carts in the book, that was real. During the Depression, people didn't have any money to buy gasoline. So they took the tires off of their old cars, and put them on their wagons, and still used their mule or horse to pull it. But it rolled better. That was a Hoover cart.

It's so multilayered. There are so many characters from every walk of life. You really feel like you are reading about a real town. The themes in the book teachers use every year to teach about prejudice and outsiders and love. Teachers have helped this book live on and on because they teach it every year, and that's how whole generations of kids read it.

It's so real, it feels so real. And it's so gentle. It talks about really hard issues, but from Scout's point of view. It's kind of a slow-moving book. You have time to think about all these things as you're reading about this town.

The movie, of course, made our courtroom famous. We say [it's] the most famous courtroom in America, because when the film rights were sold, they came to try to film here but decided the town had changed too much. We were still having court here in 1962, and they decided to build that courtroom on the soundstage at the back lot of Universal Studios. Henry Bumstead was the art designer, [and] won an Oscar for that movie. He told me that he took pictures, he measured it, and he wanted to get the proportions right. He wanted that courtroom, the one that Harper Lee grew up with. Harper Lee went to Hollywood and helped him on the set. She didn't stay, they say, for much of the filming. But Bumstead said that she would come on the set and help him with, "That's the right chair, that's the wrong table," that kind of thing. So he credits her for helping him win that Oscar.

Since the thirties, the town's spread out, that's for sure. And on Saturdays, the square's dead, which is very different. People shop elsewhere now. We have a Walmart. The downtown is some lawyers' offices, a few stores, and the post office. But in '35, everything was here. The Jitney Jungle [a supermarket Miss Stephanie mentions in the novel]—we really had one. V. J. Elmore's was a department store [where Jem bought Scout her baton]. Bedsole's was another department store. Everything was here in town. The doctors, the drugstores, dentists, even a boardinghouse.

We know that she doesn't want to meet all these people who come here. They started coming in 1960, when the book came out. We don't take any credit for the fact that we have twenty thousand people visit this town. We know why they're coming. And we understand that she decided to quit doing interviews. Everybody here knows that. So we don't tell people where she lives or really anything about her business. We just try to answer their questions about the book and about the town. Because everybody wants to know what was real and what wasn't. We try to just tell what we know about who really lived here during that time.

When I came to work here in '96, I would see Harper Lee around town. During the fall through the Christmas holidays, on into January and February, and then, sometime in the spring,

I would realize I hadn't seen her. I would hear that she had gone back to New York on the train. But she always came home for the holidays. I would look out the window, and she'd be going into the post office. She would come out with armloads of mail, go to the car, sit there and open something. She would be at the grocery store. She would go to church. She was not a recluse at all. She just wanted her privacy. So we didn't tell people, "Go here, and go there, you may see her." We just knew that she was around, and [we were] glad that she would come back to Monroeville.

There are so many people who say to me, "This is my favorite book ever." They love her. They want to tell her how much they love her. But she doesn't want that. It would be too much. So this museum is not a place that she would want to be, because they would recognize her and try to talk to her about the book.

I think she's a realist. She had to write the book. She went to New York to get it published. That was her goal. And then she wasn't prepared for the publicity, the fame. I respect the fact that she was able to step back from that. Look what happened to Truman. He loved it. He loved the attention. She decided not to do that. And so, to come to Monroeville and be able to move around the way she does here is pretty amazing.

Truman Capote's mother brought him back to Monroeville to live with the cousins who raised her. She and her brothers and sisters were orphans. He came when he was a baby and was taken care of by these old cousins. He went to the first grade, part of the second grade, and then went to New York to live with his mother, who had married Joe Capote by then. But he came back every summer to play with Nelle.

On South Alabama Street is Mel's Dairy Dream, and that was where Harper Lee grew up. Her house was torn down in 1951 or

'52 when Mister Lee sold it and Mel's Dairy Dream was built. So generations of people in Monroeville have gone there for milk-shakes and hamburgers, and still do.

The book seems so familiar, and then we assume things. I hear townspeople interchange the name of the real person and the character that they think was the model. In conversation, when they're talking about the real person, they'll use the fictional name.

Harper Lee's mother was Frances Cunningham Finch, and Frances Finch's father was the postmaster up at Finchburg, which was up near Williams Landing. He married Ellen Williams, and they lived in that area. All the stuff in the book about Finch's Landing, I relate to Williams Landing, which was a steamboat landing right there, where her family lived. Frances Cunningham Finch married A. C. Lee and moved to Monroeville. They had Alice, Louise, Ed, and Nelle. Mrs. Lee died in 1951. I'm not sure what of. Ed died in 1951 of an aneurism, they think. He was at Maxwell Air Force Base in Montgomery. So that was two deaths in their family that year, 1951.

A. B. Blass [who owned the local hardware store] says he delivered papers to Mrs. Lee, and she would be sitting out on the porch swing in the afternoon dressed in a gingham dress, like a lot of the ladies did. They finished their work in the morning. They cooked dinner, which is the noon meal, and then, in the afternoons, they would sit on the porch and visit with people.

He would take her the paper. And she'd say, "You're such a nice young man." I really haven't heard other people talk about her. Jennings Carter stayed at the Faulk house a lot and played with Truman and with Harper Lee. He remembers Mrs. Lee playing the piano.

When the book came out in 1960, I wasn't here. So I began asking people, "What did you think [when the book first came out]?" Most people said that they didn't pay it any mind. I asked my mama, and she said, "Well, it just seemed so familiar, we didn't see anything special about it."

When the movie rights were sold and Gregory Peck came to Monroeville, that's when they sat up and took notice. Everybody has a story of Gregory Peck just being here in this town, staying at the hotel, eating in the restaurants, and visiting Mister Lee. That's when people noticed the book. If Hollywood's gonna make a movie out of this book, then there's something about it that's special. One girl said that Gregory Peck came into the bank and wrote a check. She was so nervous she had a hard time giving him his money.

Some young girls rode around town trying to find him to get his autograph. He and Harper Lee were meeting at a little motel, and the girls found out where they were. They dared one another to go and knock on the door. So Martha Moorer had to go and knock on the door. And Harper Lee answered and said, "Martha Louise, what are you doing here? Leave us alone," or something like that, and started to shut the door. But Gregory Peck said, "No, it's OK. I'll give her my autograph." She cannot find that autograph, though, 'cause I asked her for a copy of it.

When the book came out in 1960, Ernestine's Book and Gift Store bought copies, and there was a signing. Everybody in town came to have their book signed. Ernestine bought five hundred copies, and they sold. One lady said, "We just were appalled that she bought that many. We didn't think that many would sell. We were afraid for her to lose money."

Now those people are bringing their books in to show me because they are valuable and rare.

I don't know a lot about her relationship with Truman. I just know how close they were when they were children. I just feel like . . . they were friends the rest of his life. Because friendships that you form when you're a kid with someone who is of like mind really do endure.

I know she wants to stay a mystery and let the book stand for itself. Half the people now who come here say, "I don't need to go and see her. I love the book. And I have the book." I see the word *recluse* in articles all the time, and that's not true. She's not a recluse. Each year we put on *To Kill a Mockingbird*, the play, and that's our big fund-raiser to keep this building intact. It's a county building, but we don't get funding from them. It was this building that Harper Lee had in mind when she wrote her book.

Allan Gurganus

Allan Gurganus was born in Rocky Mount, North Carolina, in 1947. He is the author of three novels, including, Oldest Living Confederate Widow Tells All *(1989) and* White People *(1990), and a collection of short stories,* Plays Well with Others *(1997).*

I remember the title was extremely beautiful. I thought the title was everything a title should be—an invitation, a mystery. I loved mockingbirds, and there was part of the cult of living in the South: There's always one on every corner just singing its little gullet out.

One of the things that struck me initially as someone who lived in a town of twenty-four hundred was, I felt the permission to write about small-town life and the permission to feel that huge international drama, all the circumstances of truth, justice, and the American way, could be played out in a town of two thousand souls. And could be played out by a single just man who stands up to be counted. Atticus resembled a lot of the Harvard-educated lawyers who had gone away to school and come home. Faulkner is full of those people too, who seemed in those days to be the real aristocrats, the people who could have done anything but chose not to leave, the people who had a kind of comprehensive vision of the sociology of the town and were amused by it and forgave it and defended the wrongly accused.

I was close enough to Scout's age to be attracted both to the childlikeness of the voice and the sagacity of the adult perspective. I think . . . one of the things that's not quite understood about the book is that Lee manages to be a child and an adult. The analysis of the town is very shrewd and with the wisdom of an eighty-year-old dowager who's seen it all. And yet, the voice can be very fresh and very innocent and beguiling and Huck Finn–like. I think Huck Finn and *To Kill a Mockingbird* have a lot in common, and I think Harper Lee learned a lot from Twain in terms of a child's critical vision of the hierarchy, of the system.

There was a kind of freshness. I remember reading it in one sitting as one of those books that pulls you through it. I thought it was an extraordinary book, but I was just young enough to know that there were many extraordinary books. I thought all books were extraordinary. What's marvelous is that you see that sometimes the first things that happen to you are as big as they seemed. And it's very moving to see what an evergreen and enduring achievement it's truly turned out to be.

The narrative is very tough, because she has to both be a kid on the street and aware of the mad dogs and the spooky houses, and have this beautiful vision of how justice works and all the creaking mechanisms of the courthouse. Part of the beauty is that she, Harper Lee, trusts the visual to lead her, and the sensory. You really know that courthouse extremely well, who sits where, where the black people sit, where the fans are. I think that one of the many reasons that Horton Foote wrote such an amazing screenplay is that he had the good sense to know a great thing when he found it, and he trusted it. So even the relation of Atticus to the lady down the street—who's what, his part-time lover of an evening, who knows?—is very beautiful, deftly honored. It's not spelled out, it's not oversimplified or made lurid.

I think one of the many anomalies of the book is that it is a very great book that was made into a very great film. Usually, great films are made from second-rank books, and usually great books make terrible movies. But there is something in the opening sequences of the film with the childhood toys and images of the precious things saved that lets you know you're in a child's vision, and it holds there.

I'm interested in the fact that "a Boo Radley" is now a phrase in the language. It's sort of like, "the block's Boo Radley." Many people who haven't read *To Kill a Mockingbird* have that phrase in their lingo. That's what every writer wants, to identify some previously noted but not named phenomenon and provide the English-speaking world with a brand-new word, a brand-new concept. And I think she has done that.

Calpurnia is like the black women in Carson McCullers, but she's very particular and very proud and a kind of role model. Goodness is, I think, underestimated as a dramatic virtue in fiction. Except for the white-trash villains, everybody in the town is sort of good or trying to be. I think that's one of the enduring attractions of the book. Maybe in our times, which are so full of corruption and just disgustingly forthright greed, our nostalgia for this vision of decency and the system working makes it a more important book, not a less important one.

I loved the story of Harper Lee visiting the set with Gregory Peck, and he's in his white ice-cream suit, and it's all properly creased and a little three days old, and she starts crying at the sight of him. She said, "You look just like my daddy, and especially the way your little tummy pouches out." He said, "That's not a pouch, that's great acting!"

I think it's maybe a testament to the book that Gregory Peck as a star was always a little stiff, a little angular. This movie, I think, humanized him, and he relaxed into the part because all the virtue was there and he could underplay.

I read *To Kill a Mockingbird* again two years ago, partially because a godson was reading it in high school and I wanted to seem cool in his eyes and pretend that I knew all about it in advance, so I burned the midnight oil and read it in a single sitting. I was amazed—there's dew all over it. The description early on of the ladies with their powder sort of melted like frosting on teacakes by nightfall seemed to be so knowing and so loving, and kind of rueful but very true. It's a book of a real writer.

I think [this time] I saw it more in the social context of the period. I look back at the civil rights struggle and think that if Dwight Eisenhower or Jack Kennedy had flown from Washington, during the battles for integration, and had taken the hand of a little black girl who was being pelted by tomatoes and jeered at by white crackers, and walked to school with that child, risked all their political capital to do the right thing, as Atticus would have done, the civil rights struggle would have been put forward by thirty years. But they were too cowardly, they were too mixed in their own feelings about race, they were too canny as politicians to take that chance.

When I read this book, somehow I had this vision of the biggest guy on the block taking the littlest hand on the block and leading this child to school. And it never happened. But it happened in the book, and I think that's one of the eternal attractions of the work.

Writers are known as sort of self-regarding and isolated and competitive and jealous of each other. But in my experience, writers are also each other's first readers; they are the ones to note first what you've done extremely well. If they're honest with each other, they can both grow at an extraordinarily advanced rate. I think the childhood friendship between Harper Lee and Truman Capote was clearly immensely important to each of them. They became each other's first readers, each other's best readers, each other's shrewdest judges.

I knew Capote late in his life in the old Studio 54 days, when I was a negotiable young thing who would be whisked past any velvet rope—those were the glory days—and if you weren't asked in the first time, you just took your shirt off, and that would get you in. At that time, he was near the end of his sociability, and he and Liza Minnelli and Halston and Elizabeth Taylor and all the gang were there. He had a big fedora on a little bitty man, and he was usually just totally stoned, and he was like a puff adder. I don't even know what a puff adder is, but that phrase made sense. He groped me and all the other boys in that place. It was like a little monkey going from vine to vine. For me, at that age I was just starting out and I was beginning to be published in the *New Yorker* and various places, and I knew who he was, obviously. But for me he was kind of an object lesson in what not to become. Even though we were partying at the same place, I felt very distanced from him and very sad that he would be publicly seen that stoned and that foolish. And I'm glad to say that, except for six or eight times, I've tried to avoid that trap myself.

But I think Capote's treatment of her is an indication of where his work stands in relation to hers, except for *In Cold Blood*, which had the benefit of her extraordinary legwork, her extraordinary political sense, her finesse in covering for him. I don't think any of Capote's fiction will last, in the larger sense. It lacks that ethical center that *To Kill a Mockingbird* has, and it's obviously not going to be taught to high school students.

I mean, that's not to diminish the fact that he was an extremely talented writer. But what he did with his life, he did with his work. That is to say, he went to too many parties, and he was too intent on being flown places in private jets. Unlike her, he didn't stay home; he went away.

The beauty of *In Cold Blood* is that it is about justice, but the more we know about the backstage machinations, which means that you have to execute the protagonist in order to sell the book, the more you realize that he was criminal in his treatment of his subjects.

I think she was extremely prudent in a way of disappearing the way she did. You pay a kind of price for being on call, and you get to look into the face of your readers, all of them sometimes, it seems, but there's a kind of privacy, a kind of integrity that you risk losing if you're not careful. And she had the object lesson of what Capote had done for and to himself.

When I read *To Kill a Mockingbird*, it does not seem to me like a first book, and it does not seem to me like an only book, because it seems to be the work of a born writer, not the work of a person who has an autobiographical story to tell and can only tell that one. It seems to me that she must have written books before this, even though she was thirty-five when it was published. It's a very evolved and sophisticated literary creation. And I have to believe that she must have written books after, because I know, as a writer, if I don't have a morning's work, I want to kick a cat around the block. I have to write, or I become intolerable to myself. And I don't know how you wean yourself from the habit of writing. Maybe you write only letters to fans. That's what Margaret Mitchell did after *Gone with the Wind*. She never, ever intended to write another book, though she strung her publisher along to shake him down for money. That was the one book she wrote, and it was about her grandmother. That's an example. Or Thomas Wolfe's *Look Homeward Angel*, which was by far the best thing he ever wrote. It made a huge sensation, and he continued to write. But I honestly think that if Thomas Wolfe pulled a Harper Lee and disappeared, his stock would be much higher than it is now. He wrote much too much, too [uncritically]. He has many volumes but only one book. I look at the example of Salinger, who got terrible reviews for one book—unjust reviews, we now know—and just withdrew from ever letting his work be published. But we know from local rumor that he has installed a safe-deposit vault in his study, fireproof. Now, you don't have to be Sherlock Holmes to figure out that this is a guy with sixteen books that will be published someday. I hope I'm alive to see it, because I think it would be a beautiful thing. It must be a very satisfying thing to say, "Nyeh, nyeh, I'm going to take my marbles and go home," and to continue the saga of the Glass family.

I think the circumstances of the huge success of *To Kill a Mockingbird*, winning the Pulitzer, the way Margaret Mitchell did, must have been daunting, and I can imagine drawing back and saying, "What's my next story?" I know from conversation that she was looking at a kind of murder circumstance, not unlike *In Cold Blood*, for her next material. And maybe Capote scooped her in the sense that he benefited from her reportage and clearly used some verbatim passages from her, unacknowledged, and maybe she felt that he had somehow preempted her next book. Maybe the death of her agent and her editor, maybe the burning of her writing hand—all these might have contributed to her falling quiet.

The odd thing about publishing is that you can remain a writer and cease to publish. Publishing is so jangling and so frequently hideous. You subject yourself to scrutiny from people who haven't really read your book; you're being trotted around like a dog and pony show, whether you mean it or not. I can understand how people sit home and say, "I'm going to write book after beautiful book, and they'll be found later"—as long as they have the financial security, which she was allowed by virtue of the first publication.

I don't know what writers do when they stop writing. I don't know what anybody does who is not writing. I mean, I'm sitting in traffic and I look at the person in the next car, and I honestly think, *I wonder if she's writing short stories or a novel*. Because, having done it for so many years myself, heedless of publication—I haven't had a book out in four or five years—I have beautiful things that I will someday publish, but I don't feel in any real hurry. But if I couldn't do it, I would feel like a rattlesnake with the venom backed up in me. It's a form of dreaming, it's an extra form of dreaming; it's a kind of algebraic balancing act, a kind of working out of equivalencies. And it's a place where justice can actually happen. That's one of the unacknowledged powers of the novel, is that here in this little town, in these two hundred pages, a life is saved, something is salvaged, perfect justice is achieved, however improbably. And I think that that's one of the reasons we read, is to have our faith in the process renewed.

David Kipen

David Kipen was born in Los Angeles in 1963. He was the Director of Literature for the National Endowment for the Arts (2004–2010) and supervised its Big Read program, which includes To Kill a Mockingbird. *He is a former book reviewer for the* San Francisco Chronicle.

I wish I could say that I was ten years old and it was the book that turned me on to reading. I'm sure if I had been ten, it would have. But I didn't read *To Kill a Mockingbird* until [2004], when I found out that I was going to help to run this national reading program [the Big Read] and it was going to be one of the first four books we were doing. I was grateful, because I had always meant to read it. I was half afraid that I'd waited too long, because it's a book that means a lot to people when they read it at a young age.

But I was blown away by it. I think it's a lovely, lovely book. I think it's a moral book, without being starchy or medicinal in any way. I think it's a really ennobling book and a great story and an artfully, if not infallibly, interwoven counterpointing of two stories in one.

One thing that took me a little bit by surprise and I was deeply grateful for was the humor of the book. A lot of people, when they talk about it, and including me a minute ago, tend to emphasize what an uplifting and improving book it is, and it is that. But I think maybe even more of it because it isn't written like a religious tract. It is a very funny book. Scout's voice is a very comic voice in the things she says at the expense of her schoolmates. She's a scamp and hysterically funny, and no less funny as an adult looking back, although in a slightly more fermented and seasoned way. She's just great company.

In preparing the reading materials for these cities that are reading *To Kill a Mockingbird* around the country, I edited and wrote and ghost-wrote some essays in the material, and the one phrase of my own that I hope will at least almost come back to me was that it's a book about a young girl surprised to discover her own goodness. Scout didn't quite know she was as honorable a little girl as she was until she had it shown to her and discovered her own capacity to be compassionate. So it's not reverential in the way that more didactic moral books can so often be.

At the NEA, before I even got there, they had decided that the first four books ought to be *Fahrenheit 451* and *The Great Gatsby* and *Their Eyes Were Watching God* and, of course, *To Kill a Mockingbird*. I think one of the reasons they chose that was that it's the most popular City Read book around the country. More cities for their "one city, one book" program chose *To Kill a Mockingbird* than anything else, and we figured, well, that was a sure thing.

Now that I've been to cities where they've read it, I start to see why. I went to Sioux Falls, South Dakota, and rode in the St. Patrick's Day parade with the daughter of the local City Read coordinator in a life-size papier-mâché ham costume like the one Scout wears in the Halloween scene at the end of the book. She's riding in the convertible behind me, not driving, thank heaven. People just adored the book and shared from their lives as they began to talk about it. I sat in the back of the book department of Zandbroz Variety on the main drag in Sioux Falls, bumping from one readers' circle to another and sitting in on these discussions of it, and people just seem to connect with it. It dredges up things in their own lives, their interactions across racial lines, legal encounters, and childhood. It's just this skeleton key to so many different parts of people's lives, and they cherish it, and now I know why.

I wish I could be one of these people who say, "It's churlish to want more from a woman who's already given us so much," but I'm a greedy reader, and I think a true reader has to be a greedy reader. I wanted the next book, and I will always feel cheated for not having gotten it. It would be nice, it would be lovely, and if only I could get that next book, I promise I would read it gently.

I think Harper Lee is Boo Radley. People think she's Scout; I think she's Boo Radley. In the book, they talk about why it's the humane thing to let Boo Radley alone and not shine the glare of publicity on him, because he's just not built for that. It's Sheriff Tate:

> *Maybe you'll say it's my duty to tell the town all about it and not hush it up. Know what'd happen then? All the ladies in Maycomb includin' my wife'd be knocking on his door bringing angel food cakes. To my way of thinkin', Mr. Finch, taking the one man who's done you and this town a great service an' draggin' him with his shy ways into the limelight—to me, that's a sin. It's a sin and I'm not about to have it on my head. If it was any other man it'd be different, but not this man, Mr. Finch.*

And that's Harper Lee, and it would be a sin to drag her into the limelight. I have no problem whatsoever with my own curiosity about her life. I think that's human and understandable and not to be apologized for. I feel very strongly about this, because I did my senior essay in college on the literature of—not Harper Lee—but J. D. Salinger and B. Traven, the guy who wrote *The Treasure of the Sierra Madre*, who was a lot wilier about his reclusiveness, and my favorite of all, Thomas Pynchon. These are very private writers. But I refuse to disavow my own curiosity about their lives. I won't allow it to displace my love of their writing, but one of the very most important things biographical criticism can teach is how who you are factors in to what you do, how the way you were brought up and what sort of person you are enables you to do the work that you do. Whether you are the man who wrote *Gravity's Rainbow* or the woman who wrote *To Kill a Mockingbird*, your childhood is interesting because you are this wonderful artist and that's what it grew out of.

The movie is terrific, and I think we should put a word in here for Horton Foote, because a lot of people will tell you, as good as the book is, the movie is better. He found such a lovely way to shape the story. I bow down at his altar; he is really the gold standard for the adapter's art.

Knowing a little something about Truman Capote certainly enriched the character [Dill] for me. I think she saw what fame did to a very good friend of hers. She saw how Truman Capote was overtaken by his own mythomania, and didn't want any part of that. It's hard to argue with. Capote is a guy who squandered his talent and his life. Maybe Harper Lee had it in her to write more books; that is an opportunity that she passed up. But she's managed to preserve for herself a zone of happiness and security and friends who love her and respect her privacy. So in the Monroeville happy ending sweepstakes, I think she gets the laurel over her next-door neighbor, because she made up her mind about the life she wanted to have. And when she goes, she'll go a lot less lonely than Truman Capote was.

It's a book, I think, that families enjoy reading together, which may sound like a backhanded compliment, but that's part of what we're doing with the Big Read, is trying to come up with books that people of all ages can read together, at least in the initial phases. That's too much to ask of every book, but when you find a book that does cross, not just gender and racial lines, but ages lines too, it's a very special thing, because it's an opportunity for grown-ups to read to children without having to hide their own yawns. So, in common with very few other books, I think it is a true all-ages classic. It affords a terrific opportunity to create cross-generation conversations that a lot of other good books don't.

Wally Lamb

Wally Lamb was born in 1950 in Norwich, Connecticut. A former high-school teacher and professor, he is also the author of four novels: She's Come Undone *(1992),* I Know This Much Is True *(1998),* The Hour I First Believed *(2008), and* Wishin' and Hopin': A Christmas Story *(2009). Lamb is the editor of the nonfiction anthologies* Couldn't Keep It to Myself: Testimonies from Our Imprisoned Sisters *(2003) and* I'll Fly Away *(2007), collections of autobiographical essays that evolved from a writing workshop Lamb teaches at a maximum-security prison for women.*

I think I was about fourteen or fifteen. I didn't love reading at that age. I read because I had to for school projects, and a book report was coming due, and I'd already read the shortest books I know—*Animal Farm* and *The Red Pony*. So I happened to go into my sister's room, and she'd been yapping about this novel that she had just read that she'd liked, *To Kill a Mockingbird*. And I picked the thing up, and there's a Technicolor picture of Gregory Peck and some little girl in overalls on the cover. I flipped it open and read the first couple of sentences and two days later I, the pokiest reader I knew, had finished the book. It was the first time in my life that a book had sort of captured me. That was exciting; I didn't realize that literature could do that.

I did feel kidnapped by that book because I was in Maycomb, Alabama, with those characters, and my life around me just sort of blurred and I just kept turning those pages because I had to.

I probably didn't read it again until I was about twenty-one. I had bounced out of college and had gone right back to the high school that I had attended. I was an English teacher, and I remembered that *To Kill a Mockingbird* was a book that I had loved and also been drawn to emotionally. And I thought, *Well, I'll try it with the kids.*

And I remember working first of all with a group of slower learners, and I'm thinking, *I don't know, these opening passages are maybe a little bit of a hurdle to jump over,* but I read that part aloud and then gave the kids an assignment. And little by little, one by one, over the next week or so, it grabbed them. It was probably the first time for a lot of those kids that they became impassioned about a book. There were some pretty heated arguments about characters' motivations and who said what and why they had said it.

The most exciting thing when you're dealing with students is that the kids began to apply it to their own lives and their own observations, and then we were golden. I taught that book just about every year. I taught high school for twenty-five years, and just about every year, I did *To Kill a Mockingbird* with students. It was a book they read because they wanted to, not because they had to. So it cast the same spell for my students as it had for me.

For a lot of kids, it's the voice of Scout. It's certainly not the adult voice of Jean Louise Finch. It's Scout's voice. I think the fact that she is a tomboy helps the boys. A lot of the guys, as I recall, liked Jem, too. He sort of spoke their kind of language, and a lot of them had annoying little sisters, so that invited them along for the ride as well.

This was in the seventies, when I started teaching, and there was a lot of racial turmoil in the country. Because the characters become sort of personally applicable, I think a story can go a lot further lots of times than a headline can or something on the six-thirty news. So for the kids, I think it became sort of a vehicle by which they could begin to think and sort of process some of these emotional reactions that they were having.

I know one of the things that happened at our high school during that early era when I was teaching was that the African-American kids were demanding a black history course. And the school was not providing one, so the kids staged a demonstration out on the green near the school. I was thinking about this just today. I think, in its own way, *To Kill a Mockingbird*—and I don't mean to overstate this—sort of triggers the beginning of change and certainly puts onto the stage the questions of racial equality and bigotry in the way, a century earlier, Harriet Beecher Stowe's *Uncle Tom's Cabin* sort of stirred things up and got people riled up enough and motivated to change things.

And then, of course, [there is] the inevitable exploitation of a book that means so much to so many people. I know a little bit about Harriet Beecher Stowe because she lived close by, in Hartford. And I know that she was sort of appalled by some of these really cheesy stage productions that started traveling the country. And I saw at one point, maybe three or four years ago up in Montpellier, Vermont, a staged version of *To Kill a Mockingbird*. It was OK. I wouldn't say it was cheesy. But it couldn't even approach that same kind of experience that reading the book is.

The movie, I sort of go back and forth about. When I was teaching high school, the big treat at the end was to see the movie, and it was fun to talk about the choices that a director makes and casting and all that.

So as is often the case when you see the film version of a book that you loved, I really didn't like it. I loved the performances. I loved the casting of the main characters. I was appalled at some of the casting of the minor characters—Miss Maudie, and Bob Ewell I didn't think looked nearly as grungy as he should have. But also, there were several other characters who had been edited out—Mrs. Dubose, for one.

That for me is one of the most wrenching chapters of the novel. When I was teaching books like *To Kill a Mockingbird* year after year, I was beginning to get interested myself in the underpinnings of how novels work. And that was one of the books that really taught me how to write fiction myself, and I remember vividly the description of Mrs. Dubose in the pain of withdrawal. She puts a finger to her mouth and draws it back and has that sort of string of spittle that goes with it. Man, that's writing! When Jem freaks out and trashes the flowers that she loves so much, that's a dramatic scene.

The novel was really instructive. It's beautiful literature, but it's also a great course in how to write a novel, I think.

I use *To Kill a Mockingbird* with my inmate students. I do some volunteer teaching in a women's prison; I teach writing. And I'll use models from *Mockingbird*, particularly when I want to talk about sensual language and how you can evoke emotion and re-action through the use of the five senses.

There's that gorgeous description of Maycomb at the begin-ning where she says:

> *Maycomb was an old town, but it was a tired old town when I first knew it. In rainy weather the streets turned to red slop; grass grew on the sidewalks, the courthouse sagged in the square. Somehow, it was hotter then: a black dog suffered on a summer's day; bony mules hitched to Hoover carts flicked flies in the sweltering shade of the live oaks on the square. Men's stiff collars wilted by nine in the morning. Ladies bathed before noon, after their three-o'clock naps, and by nightfall were like soft teacakes with frostings of sweat and sweet talcum.*

Now, I teach my students that, forget the adjectives, it's all about the verbs: "flicked flies," "sagged in the square," "sweltered in." It's all there. It is a one-paragraph course on writing. Writ-ers evoke things that readers can see and hear, but I think those tactile sensations, like "soft teacakes with frostings of sweat," those kinds of things—that's real writing, that's literature. Now, is it sustained throughout the novel? Not necessarily. But it's doing other things at different times. So I think it's a wonderful model.

On some level at least, I think I understand [why Harper Lee hasn't published another book]. I wrote my first novel, *She's Come Undone*, over ten years. I was teaching high school at the time; I was getting up on weekends, rising at four o'clock and driving up to the all-night study room at the local university and writing in longhand. I did that over a number of years. So nine years later I had a novel, and I didn't think it was going to be published. But then it was, and I was flabbergasted. It was published in 1992. Then in 1997 I got a call from Oprah Winfrey saying, "Gee, we love this book, and we would like to feature it in this book club we're doing." So that was wonderful. It was a crazy, wild, and wonderful ride. Suddenly this book that had a little modest success by "Wally who?" hit the top of the charts fueled by the Oprah book-club thing. I'd been working for about six years on a second novel [*I Know This Much Is True*]; the following year it was ready. Lo and behold, Oprah picks that one for the book club as well. So, as great as that was, as exciting, the way that it gave me a much wider stage and millions more readers than I might have had otherwise, I have found that in the writing of my third novel, it's been somewhat intimidating to do because of the reception of the first two novels.

Now, I have no idea whether Harper Lee struggled against that kind of stuff. I just know that it does change the equation when people are waiting for a novel or writing you letters saying, "Aren't you done yet?" So every sentence becomes something that you worry about. The best days for me as a writer are the days when I can get up from the desk and open the door of my office and chase everyone's expectations out of the room and just write it for myself. But that doesn't always happen.

Harper Lee had, I believe, role models throughout her life— people who were giving her the message that books mattered. And I think that sort of seeped into your bones after a while. For me it wasn't like that. But I think, from what I know, that was the case.

And then, of course, she had her friend Truman Capote, who was also doing it. I would guess probably that when they were kids they might have been shooting stories back and forth and telling stories collaboratively.

I believe Capote's first fiction was published prior to *To Kill a Mockingbird*. So then she gets to see what that's like, I would imagine that provides even more motivation, because here's not only an author who has a book but somebody I know.

Atticus Finch is certainly a paragon. He's a model that we can all aim toward. In a sense, he is so perfect, and I understand that she modeled the character somewhat on her own father. And, of course, I don't buy for a minute that anyone's father, my own included, or me as a father, has achieved that kind of perfection, is always spot-on in terms of what to say and what to fight for. But I imagine [her father] must have been a wonderful man, and certainly the book does seem like a tribute to some really fine values. And fighting when you need to fight.

I started writing fiction late in my life. I was about thirty years old, and most fiction writers start a lot earlier. Very early on, I slammed into the wall of all I didn't know about how to write fiction. So I entered a program at Vermont College. It was a Master in Fine Arts program in writing, and I had the good fortune of working with a wonderful teacher named Gladys Swan—great writer, terrific teacher. Gladys has these big thick, Coke-bottle-bottom glasses that, I mean, whatever she says, it sounds like the oracle, it looks like the oracle is speaking to you, and in a sense she was. She said to me, "Wally, what would you like to get out writing fiction?" I hadn't even asked myself that question, so I had to sort of wing it and make up an answer. I said, 'Well, *To Kill a Mockingbird* is a novel I love, and it's a novel I don't have to work overtime to teach. The kids slip into the stream and allow the story to take them where it takes them. I guess probably my goal would be to write the kind of fiction that teenagers would want to read." And Gladys frowned at that, and she said, "Well my dear, the first thing that I have to tell you is, Don't prejudge who your audience is going to be. Don't write fiction for teenagers or for anybody else. Write it for yourself. Write to explore what you need to explore. Write it to satisfy you, and then send it out, and whoever needs it will find it."

That proved to be wonderful advice for me. And I came, over the years, to the realization that I bet is true of Harper Lee as well. You start with who and what you know. You take a survey of the lay of the land that formed you and shaped you. And then you begin to lie about it. You tell one lie that turns into a different lie. And after awhile, those models sort of lift off and become their own people rather than the people you originally thought of.

And when you weave an entire network of lies, what you're really doing, if you're aiming to write literary fiction, what you're really doing is, by telling lies you are trying to arrive at a deeper truth. Your work is no longer factual, but it's true. It's true not only for you and your own experience, your singular experience, but it also hopefully becomes true for other people. And your readers are nourished by that.

The opening passages are kind of difficult for high school kids. There's some pretty highfalutin language there that can be roadblocks for kids, particularly kids who don't like to read. And beginnings of books often are hard to get past. So when I was teaching high school, what I would very often do is read some of those first passages and get past the history of Maycomb County. The novel, of course, starts with Scout's voice, but then it sort of becomes the adult Jean Louise, who is filling you in, giving you the exposition. But when Scout's voice kicks in in earnest and begins to tell you the story of what began that summer and ended three years later, then the kids are OK. What they do is, they dip their foot into the water, and then they ease into the stream, and the story and the language, and the voice in particular, take them down a smooth ride. And then you don't have to worry about whether or not they're doing the assignments; they're reading voluntarily and jumping forward, so you say, "Read chapters twelve and thirteen for tomorrow," and they'll finish the book.

Scout's a blast. I love the fact that she's a little smart-ass. I love the fact that she can be self-deprecating. I enjoy the fact that she speaks first with her fists and then has to sort of back up three to four steps. She's, in a sense—and I haven't really thought too much about this—but she's sort of an extension of a Huck Finn character. Of course, we love Huck for those same reasons. I think she's very typically an American character in that she's poking at the boundaries of good taste, and what's proper. I love some of scenes between Scout and Aunt Alexandra because she debunks a lot of that phony baloney stuff in ways that readers just love.

Alice Finch Lee

Alice Finch Lee, Harper Lee's older sister, was born in Bonifay, Florida, in 1911. She has been practicing law at Barrett, Bugg & Lee in Monroeville, Alabama, since 1944.

*M*y father was totally a self-made person. Back in those days, they didn't have much rural education. He probably went to a school less than a year, all told. But he was one of the best-educated men you ever knew. By sixteen he had read himself, educated himself, and he took the teacher's examination and taught school at sixteen. His family were all farmers, and my father was determined not to be a farmer. He took math and became an accountant, and he began to get jobs. My father became a bookkeeper for sawmill companies, and he moved around wherever. He came to Monroe County and was bookkeeper for a big sawmill down in a place called Manistee. My father eventually began to keep books for a sawmill company in Finchburg. That's where my mother lived. That's where they met. Then my father and mother were married in 1910 and lived in Florida, where he was keeping books for a mill down there, and I was born there. I am the only alien in the family, the only one not born in Alabama.

When I was growing up, [Monroeville] was an all-Protestant community, and now it's not. We have a flourishing Catholic church. That is one of the differences. When I was growing up, we didn't have things like the golf course. By the time I was an adult, we had the beginnings of a golf course, which was at the same time used as a landing field for planes to come in. Back in those days, we didn't have sewers. We had to go to separate facilities to go to the bathroom. And when I was in the fourth grade, a young boy in my room had been excused [to go to the bathroom]. He rushed back in the building and said, "Something is flying around out there." And with one accord the whole fourth grade rushed out. And there was a plane circling over. And that was the first airplane I could ever remember seeing.

I grew up riding trains. I loved to ride a train. To this day, if they had them, I'd ride them. There were no bridges over the Delta. The railroads were our arteries of transportation. Now when my mother grew up out in the country, the Alabama River was their highway.

Nelle Harper and I were fifteen years apart. We had different childhoods. I was an only child for nearly five years, and I wasn't too happy when our little sister [Louise] was born. But I adjusted to that. And then, nearly five years later our little brother [Edwin] was born. And then, almost five years later, my baby sister, Nelle Harper, was born. So we grew up almost like only children. We were not companions for each other until we were adults.

When I went to college, she was just learning to walk. I was gone during that early part. Then I came home and stayed here until 1937. She was growing up then. She was a very young child. Despite people wanting to make *To Kill a Mockingbird* a biography or an autobiography or a true story, we had a mother. We loved both parents.

Nelle Harper grew up quite the little tomboy. The nearest child to her was the brother [Edwin], and he was definitely the big brother, even though that gap was between them. Where we lived there were no small children in the immediate neighborhood when Nelle Harper was born. Most of the people who were growing up there were my contemporaries and not small children. Back in those days, we did not have problems that people face today, and children could go where they wanted within reason.

The Christmas that Nelle Harper was going to be ten, all she wanted was a bicycle. Now, my sister Louise was going to be married on the day after Christmas. Nelle Harper was ten years old. Louise was leaving home. Nelle Harper wanted to know for sure she was getting that bicycle. So she had gone all around to all the merchants and places that carried a bicycle, and she could not find that Mr. or Mrs. Lee had bought a bicycle. She was very disgusted. She was convinced she was not going to get the bicycle for Christmas. So she just said, disgustedly, "Nobody's having a Christmas except Weezie. She's getting a husband." So she was very downcast. Christmas morning, when she found that bicycle under the tree, she couldn't believe she had it. She just got on that bicycle and took off, and we didn't see too much of her during the rest of the day.

At home we were pretty much allowed to go in the direction we wanted to go, unless we were headed the wrong way. But we knew we were expected to go to Sunday school and church on Sunday, which we did. We knew we had to go elementary, high school, whatever it is, through the week. But we were pretty much left on our [own] resources for entertainment.

Nelle Harper was very athletic. She liked to play with the little boys more than the little girls because she liked to play ball. She played football with them, baseball with them, and that was gone when she got up into junior high. But as I said, this was during the Depression, and children basically did not have many store-bought toys. They made their own recreations, and it was not difficult to do.

When I was little, I was a great paper-doll cutter-outer. We would order paper catalogues and make paper-doll furniture out of it. We would have whole paper dollhouses and paper dolls to reside, families and that. Maybe several of us in the neighborhood would go together and do this. I was never much in sports. Not interested, except as a bystander. I liked to watch ball.

I was a child of the Depression. After my first year of college,

I had to stop. I came home and worked. There were no jobs around. People think this is the first time our country's ever been through anything like this. But I can assure them there has been another time like it. I worked at the *Monroe Journal*. In fact, my father and I bought it and I worked there until '37. I wanted to go back to school. I got a job in Birmingham at the Internal Revenue. That was the year Social Security had become law, and this whole Department of Social Security was being created as a part of IRS. So I went to Birmingham and I finished pre-law at night. I started taking it, not with the idea of finishing. I started for the improvement of skills in my job, as a number of people that work in IRS did. When I had done a couple of years of that, I had gotten hooked on wanting to go on to law school. So I finished law school there. I was in Birmingham seven years. Nelle Harper was growing up in those years, and during the war years, people who worked for the government were not allowed to use public transportation, and gasoline was rationed. I didn't get home too often. I took the bar the summer of '43 and passed it. My father asked me at that time if I were interested in coming home and practicing with him. He wasn't pushing or anything. He was just being like he'd always been: "Do your own thing, but do it well." And I said I would have to have two questions answered. And Daddy said, "What are they?" And I said, The first one is, when you grow up in one town, you are always Mr. Lee's little girl. Would I be an adult separate and apart from you?" And my father said, "I think you've been gone long enough for that not to happen." And I said, "The second thing is, how is a small town going to react to a woman in a law office?" There were not many around in those days. And my father smiled and said, "You'll never know until you've tried it." And I decided to try it.

When I came home to build a practice, everybody knew I worked for IRS. They all assumed I'd do income tax. I'd never had done any [income tax] but make my own. Back in those days, not everybody had had to file an income tax. But the government had come up with a Victory tax, which taxed everything above $600. So everybody had to file something. I was of use with people wanting to file income taxes. I didn't have to depend on Daddy's practice.

My brother was in the service. He wanted to be in the Air Force, and because he was not twenty-one, which was the age of maturity back in those days, he could not go in without my father's permission. Daddy wanted him to finish school and then go in, but the youngsters back in those days were just absolutely on their ear to get into the Air Force. Ed was in college at Auburn. Finally my father said, "Go ahead and take the test for the Air Force, and if you pass, I'll sign it. But if you don't pass, you'll go back to school and finish your degree." Ed failed to pass. He thought he was the perfect specimen, but back then they didn't take anybody with any little injury. Ed had injured a knee when he played football, and while it didn't bother him and he was not crippled, he wasn't perfect. So he went ahead and enlisted as a private from Monroe County so he would be counted against this county's quota. Then right after that, they sent him to Miami to go to officer's training school, at which time he would come back to Auburn and get his commission.

Well, when he'd been in Miami for six weeks, they picked him up and sent him to Harvard. He didn't finish his OTS [officer training school]. He was to go to Harvard for six weeks and be trained as a statistical officer, then go back to Miami and finish his OTS. Well, they didn't let him go back. When he got through at Harvard, they gave him his commission as a second lieutenant, shipped him over to San Francisco, presumably to go to the Pacific. He had been at sea about three days. They called the ship back, and it put in at Seattle. They removed about four young men from the ship, and my brother was one of those. The ship went on the way it was headed. My brother was shipped back to New York to sail for England. He had literally covered the four corners of the United States in the process of getting his commission.

Well, a statistical officer did not fly. He was not a pilot, but he could fly if there was space on anything. He got to England, and he had ways of letting us know where he was through the censor. He wrote one letter and made reference to Chaucer, so of course we knew where he was in England. I remember one time when he was in France, in his letter he said, "Do you remember that little redheaded Fleming girl in Monroeville? That was Nancy." There were ways that he could communicate with us and let us know where he was. He was with the Mustang group, the 354th fighter pilot outfit that flew the Mustangs. Mustangs wiped themselves out of business. They were the fastest things that could go with the bombers for protection. Eventually, as the war went on, and after D-day, and the bombers could get closer and closer to Berlin, they did not need the protection. So they wiped themselves out of a job, literally. So when the war was over in England, Ed expected to be shipped to the West, to the Pacific, but VJ Day came quicker than they could get him over there. So he finally got out of [the] service, came home, finished college, married, had two children and then died of an aneurism in his sleep. He had been called back up into service when the Korean thing was on the way. He was in Maxwell Air Force Base in Montgomery waiting to see where he was going to be shipped when he died of the aneurism. His daughter was three years old and his son was nine months old. His son is a local dentist now. And his daughter lives in Alexander City.

Nelle Harper had a vivid imagination all of her life, and early on she would compose stories. Daddy gave her an old beat-up typewriter, and she typed that way [gesturing hunt-and-peck method] the rest of her life. She never knew anything but the hunt-and-peck system, but she could go quite well with that.

I think in the back of her mind the idea [to be a writer] was there, not necessarily expressed. But in college she went to law school because she thought the disciplines of law were good training for somebody writing. She never intended to practice law.

I read the manuscript and OK'd it. I thought it was very good but was surprised by the reception it got. [I don't have a favorite part]; I just look at the book as a whole.

After the manuscript had gone for publication, my father had a heart attack, and Nelle Harper was down here. Then after that, she went to Kansas with Truman Capote to help him research the Clutter murders out there, and that was just on the eve of the publication. *Mockingbird* had not hit the stands when she was out there the first time. When they went back the second time, *Mockingbird* was beginning to do quite well.

Here was this little boy next door, here was this little girl next door, and they played together a lot. I've known Truman Capote's mother's side of the family, not his father's side.

When [Truman's grandparents] married, they had five children. The youngest of the children fell off a horse, took pneumonia, and died. The young mother grieved herself to death, and there was nobody to take these children, so a bunch of cousins, three old-maid sisters and one brother, unmarried, who were living at the house next door to us in the neighborhood, took all of those children and reared them and educated them. The oldest of all of them was Truman's mother [Lillie Mae Faulk]. She went to Normal School and met Archie Persons and married him.

Archie Persons was very highly educated and very smart, but did not use his mind to make his living. Then Lillie Mae eventually went to New York and met Joe Capote, and once she married him, they took Truman to New York permanently.

Some of the other descendants of Truman's cousins still live around here, and they have tried to promote Truman and his ancestry. They had as much imagination as Truman. You'd get the strangest ideas about how they grew up over the years. Nelle and I have had hysterics over how they said the Faulks lived.

Truman became very jealous because Nelle Harper got a Pulitzer and he did not. He expected *In Cold Blood* to bring him one, and he got involved with the drugs and heavy drinking and all. And that was it. It was not Nelle Harper dropping him. It was Truman going away from her.

My father lived until April of 1962, so he was here when it came out and when she won the Pulitzer. He knew about that. He was a very proud father, a very proud father.

Nelle Harper says that everybody around Monroeville was determined to see themselves in the book. They would go do anything—come up to her and say, "I'm so-and-so in the book." One day, for instance, a lady in town said to me, "I am so glad Nelle Harper put my aunt Clara in the book." And I thought to myself, *Who could be Aunt Clara in the book*? And I said, "Verna, what makes you think that?"

"Because one of her characters used the same expression that my aunt used." That was typical. People wanted to be in the book.

But wherever people read it, we learned that wherever they were, they placed the book setting where they lived. Early on, she got a letter from a young woman in Chicago who was a doctor, and she said, "I'm interested to know when you spent so much time in Greensborough." Now Greensborough is not too far from Tuscaloosa, and the only time Nelle Harper had ever been to Greensborough was when she passed through to go to school.

In New York, Nelle could move around without being recognized. Her attitude was, the kind of recognition that was coming out was the kind that was placed on entertainers who *wanted* to be recognized—who promoted it for their business reasons. She did not think that a writer needed to be recognized in person, and it bothered her when she got too familiar.

When she was in New York, right after the publication, she granted some interviews. But as time went on, she said that reporters began to take too many liberties with what she said. And what they would print would be apparently what they wanted rather than what she said. So she just wanted out. And she started that and did not break her rule. She felt like she'd given enough.

You know, when wrong things get in print, they circulate forever. No way to retract them successfully.

She didn't put herself under the burden of writing like she did when she was doing *Mockingbird*. But she continued to write something. I think she was just working on maybe short things with an idea of incorporating them into something. She didn't talk too much about it. She says you couldn't top what she had done.

She told one of our cousins who asked her: "I haven't anywhere to go but down."

We are not very much alike, except we are both old. We both love to read. Nelle Harper loves British literature; I've stuck more with American. More biography and history. It is so intriguing in biography to put things together.

James McBride

James McBride was born in New York in 1957. He is the author of a memoir, The Color of Water: A Black Man's Tribute to His White Mother *(1996), and two novels,* Miracle at St. Anna *(2003) and* Song Yet Sung *(2008). He is the screenwriter of* Miracle at St. Anna, *a film directed by Spike Lee. McBride is a composer, plays the tenor saxophone, and performs in jazz clubs.*

I first read *To Kill a Mockingbird* when I was about twelve or thirteen years old. I read a tattered copy in my house, in New York, in Jamaica, Queens. It was just beat-up, it had no cover. The page that says what edition it was, it was all ripped. It was dog-eared and it was yellowed and in my house. When I say dog-eared, that meant a dog might have had a go at it. My brothers and sisters and I read books all the time; we weren't allowed to watch that much television anyway. I thought it was an extraordinary book. I related to a lot of the characters, and it was the first time I read a book by a white writer who really discussed the issues of racism in any way that was complicated and sophisticated. Although I wasn't sophisticated enough to understand all of the issues that were discussed, the characters were so strong and the story was so strong that I related to the characters and to the story. It was a great book. It was a book I've read many times since that tattered edition that I found in my house.

I read a lot of it in one sitting. In my house there was no peace. I grew up with eleven brothers and sisters. A lot of the reading that I did, I did in the closet or in a corner somewhere, or late at night when everyone else was asleep. It wasn't a school assignment. It was just a book that I found on my brother David's bookshelf. He had all these odd books there that would make their way around. In my house, if you had a book, you had to hold on to it, because you could get to page 175 and then it would vanish, and you wouldn't get it back, ever. So I held on to it tight until I was done.

Honesty and truth last. My initial response was more or less the same as how I read it now professionally. The writer was very forthright and spoke with great clarity about issues that I think we have a hard time discussing even today. Later, when I penned my own book, the whole business of a child looking at racism and socioeconomic classism from the prism of that child's innocence is something that I adapted for *The Color of Water*. That child's innocence is important in terms of allowing us to see the world from behind the child's eyeballs. One nice thing for me is that often people compare *The Color of Water* to *To Kill a Mockingbird*. That's great. That to me is the highest compliment.

The character description and construction in *To Kill a Mockingbird* is really the ceiling against which great character writing will forever bump, in a lot of ways. The characters are so strong and definitive, yet they have a great deal of ambiguity, and they have a great deal of innocence and then soiled innocence. They have a great deal of obvious depth and they are swept by the events of their time. Which brings to mind one thing that I've always found odd about the description of Harper Lee by other writers. They describe her as a very brave writer because she wrote about these subjects. I think she's a brilliant writer. I think Martin Luther King was brave; Malcolm X was brave; James Baldwin, who was gay and black in America and who had to move to France was brave. I think that by calling Harper Lee brave you kind of absolve yourself of your own racism. What writers are standing up now at this time when we've attacked Iraq, killed thousands and thousands of people, not to mention thousands of our own? I don't recall any great sweep of fiction writers other than maybe E. L Doctorow and Paul Auster, a couple of others, who, when it counted, stood up and said, *I'm a writer, this is who I represent, this is what I feel, this is what's right*. So, by calling her brave, we kind of absolve ourselves of our own responsibility. She certainly set the standard in terms of how some of these issues need to be discussed, but in many ways I feel the bar's been lowered, the moral bar's been lowered. And that is really distressing. We need a thousand Atticus Finches.

As an adult, it occurs to me that the black characters in the book, heroic as they are, they don't survive. The societal violence that takes place to Tom Robinson affects his family for generations, at least fictionally. In real life, my wife's great-grandfather was shot while he was standing in line to get feed, because a white guy just told him to move and he wouldn't move. That murder just goes on and on; it's told to generations of people in my wife's family. And similarly in Harper Lee's book, that part of the story was something that for me has never been quite resolved in the manner that I would like to have seen it resolve. That wasn't her purpose, to tell Tom Robinson's story, but that's partially my purpose as a writer.

I think the challenge that she laid out for us, the writers who follow in her wake, is to make sure that the various dimensions of these stories are told properly, and that we stand up in our own time to talk about issues that count now. It's easy to poke fun and say, "I would have done this," or "What a brave women she was," and so on and so forth, but when it counted, Harper Lee did what was necessary. And how many of us now are doing what's necessary in terms of standing up for the good and for the just?

She wrote about what she knew, but that doesn't absolve her of the responsibility of handling the character Tom better. Look, I wish I'd written the book, so let that be said. I'm not criticizing her work. She's a great writer. She's an American treasure, there's no question about it. But just like anything else, when the imprint of racism lays its hand on you, you have to be conscious as to how that affects you and your work. I think she did the best she could, given how she was raised. That still doesn't absolve the book or this country of the whole business of racism.

I love Calpurnia as a character, but what's her daughter's

name? I think she was a wonderful character, but you always live in that tight space when you're black. Harper Lee's approach gave Calpurnia some dimension. Calpurnia had a deep understanding of these issues, although she was restricted in terms of what she could do about a lot of these things.

I met Kurt Vonnegut before he died, and I was asking him, because his black characters were like Harper Lee's in the sense that they were really magnetic and very powerfully written and multidimensional, at least to a degree. And I said, "How do you write with such authority about black people?" And he said, "Well, my parents weren't always around, and so I was raised by a black woman who was very near and dear to me." So he took that into his work. I don't know that Harper Lee had the same experience, but her work reflects a familiarity with black folks that's more than you'd find here in New York or in Philadelphia. Our Southern brothers have had that experience of growing up together, and while there's some distance between them, there's also a lot of common ground.

Who are the real separate ones in our society, those who claim to "know your pain" or those who have been your fellow citizens, for whom you have changed a flat tire, who've changed your flat tires? In that regard, I appreciate what Harper Lee has done. I appreciate what she's done in every respect. When my daughter was in ninth grade honors English, she had to read Margaret Mitchell's book *Gone with the Wind*. How do you explain to a thirteen-year-old girl a book that depicts blacks as rapists and white-women chasers and savage people? How to explain that to a ninth grader? And what are you saying to them when that book is your honors English reading for the summer? On the other hand, when she read *To Kill a Mockingbird*, it's a book that she really liked. She could relate to it, as tragic as it is, and as difficult as it was for her to read.

Margaret Mitchell is not the writer that Harper Lee is. Harper Lee writes with the greatest clarity and a superb amount of detail, superb amount of plot, character, content, all the kind of stuff that you need to push a book forward.

People are going to be reading Harper Lee as long as people draw oxygen in this country, and they should. *To Kill a Mockingbird* [is] a great book now, it was a great book yesterday, and it will be a great book tomorrow. Whoever writes whatever in the *New Yorker* magazine or whatever, it'll be tomorrow's fish wrap. It is a great book.

If sentimentality can't be literature, my response to that is like, *dippity do dah, dippity ay*. Send a copy of Dr. Seuss's *The Sneeches*. The sneeches, after awhile they don't know who's the sneech, their identities are all spinning around in a circle. *To Kill a Mockingbird* is not overly sentimental. It's just a clear vision of what America was at that particular time, when people were filled with hope, ambiguity, love, compassion, anger, rage, everything.

I think it's not fair to lob darts and grenades at a work like this that was written with the hope that people would see what the possibilities are in this country. It's unfair at a time when you can walk into any major bookstore and 95 percent of what you see is just really wasted trees. I just can't imagine that someone would think that *To Kill a Mockingbird* isn't anything but a great American work. Really.

She didn't need a mother in that book. It would have probably soiled the book somewhat. And that's a complicated character to deal with in the South, particularly at that time: White female characters—they were restricted in many ways.

It is the metamorphosis of this young girl, evolving from a child to a girl to an almost woman as a result of her experiences without a mother—though she had neighbors who cared, and she had Calpurnia, as well. Yeah, that's a difficult one, though, because Calpurnia would be the one who people would target and say, "Here we go, you know, it's the stereotypical black mammy. I mean, how many of these do we need?" But first of all, it's rooted in reality, and secondly, it worked.

When the writer gets to the mainland, nobody asks how they got there. No one cares how William Faulkner wrote; they just know that he wrote. So who cares if you got there on the *Titanic*, or you paddled with a boat, or you jumped from lily pad to lily pad? You got to the mainland, and that's what counts.

If you only have one solo to play, then play the one solo. Why come back again and dance again? Why come back and hit the stage again? You've already branded the stage to ashes. You've killed it!

One time John Coltrane and Miles Davis were playing in one of the clubs in New York City, and John Coltrane was taking the solo, and he just kept soloing and soloing. Miles finally walked off the stage. And then Miles is meandering, waiting for Coltrane to finish; he smokes a cigarette, and Coltrane's still playing. Finally, Coltrane is finished, and Miles comes back onstage, and they finish the song, and then he turns to Coltrane and says, "Why are you playing so long?" And Coltrane says, "I don't know, Miles. I just can't seem to stop once I get started." And Miles says, "Why don't you try taking the horn out of your mouth?" And so, maybe this is Harper Lee just taking the horn out of her mouth.

There's another Coltrane story that's more relevant. Coltrane, towards the end of his life, was touring Europe. And he was soloing. And during the middle of a solo, he put his horn down and started beating his chest and singing and shouting. And so after they played, the drummer—I think his name was Rashid Ali—he went up to Coltrane, he said, "John, what's the matter? What's wrong with you, why'd you do that?" And Coltrane said, "There was nothing else to play on the horn." Maybe for Harper Lee there was nothing else to play. She sang the song, she played the solo, and she walked off the stage. And we're all the better for it. We're very grateful to her for the amount of love that she's given us.

If you're going to say something, let it be that. I wish I could do that. If I could afford to do it, if I weren't compelled to write, I would say *The Color of Water* would be where I stop. It's easy for one to leave behind what you've already done. You've planted the garden, the tomatoes have grown, and you eat them, and they come back again next year if you're lucky. There's nothing as terrible as the comedian who tells the same joke twice. Tell the joke, get off the stage, and move on. She told the story that we needed to hear. Unfortunately, it's as relevant now as it was decades ago when she first penned the book.

And interestingly enough, the book still has the kind of lean muscle that is missing from so much of the fiction that we read now. A lot of it had to be true. You can't make that kind of stuff up. If you made it up, someone would say it's not believable. So that's what separates her book from that of many other great Southern writers.

It is a difficult business, to write, and it is difficult business to really throw your heart on the page and dissect what is real and present it to people. It's kind of like ripping half your arteries out. So if she spends the rest of her life, whatever's left of it, just repairing from that one great shout, then amen. Amen to that.

The movie doesn't have the power of the book. It's a wonderful movie. Gregory Peck is a wonderful actor. I even met Brock Peters later in life. But the movie just doesn't have the resonance and the depth of the book. That is one reason why *The Color of Water* hasn't been made into a film yet. Because every time I see *To Kill a Mockingbird* as a film, I say to myself, *This is nothing; this has not one fifth of the resonance and depth of the book.* And so *The Color of Water* may never become a film, not while I'm living. Maybe my kids might want to option it out, but for me, I doubt if it'll ever be made into a movie. And that's part of the reason, because I saw what was done with *To Kill a Mockingbird*. And that was a pretty credible job by a great cast.

The problem [is] when you start talking about the characters like Calpurnia, who basically vanishes during the movie, and even Brock Peters's depiction of Tom, which was really well done. You know, Atticus Finch comes off as a liberal who is trying to do that right thing. I've had my fill of liberals who are trying to do the right thing.

Atticus Finch was a citizen in a town who saw wrong and moved to right it, despite what his neighbors thought. It was beyond him trying to do the right thing. He knew God was watching, and he was trying to get to heaven. Gregory Peck, who really was a civil rights advocate, did a wonderful job with what was handed to him, with the script that he had. But I don't think that you can deal with the complexities of the book in film. You just can't do it.

Boo Radley comes off as like a zombie, when in fact Boo Radley is anything but that. The whole business of Boo Radley in his house, by the way, is just brilliant stuff. Copied and emulated by writers everywhere, the haunted house on the block. It's a classic childhood theme, but not for black people. Yeah, we had the spooky house on our block too. But we had the spooky cops who would stop us on the way to school when you had your flute and open up your case. "What's in your flute case?" But in general, it is a classic childhood theme. Unfortunately there's always a *but* when it involves black folks.

Still, what other writer during that time was willing to take on this subject with the kind of honesty and integrity that she did. What other white writer? I can't think of anyone.

Diane McWhorter

Diane McWhorter grew up in the fifties and sixties in Birmingham, Alabama. She is the author of Carry Me Home: Birmingham, Alabama: The Climactic Battle of the Civil Rights Revolution, *which won the Pulitzer Prize in 2002, and* Dream of Freedom *(2004), a young-adult history of the civil rights movement.*

My first experience of *To Kill a Mockingbird* was actually the movie, which came out when I was in fifth grade and really too young to have read the novel. So the experience of reading the book was superimposed on the movie, which made it extra magical because it kind of reinterpreted what was by then a major part of my identity.

The movie was probably the most vivid memory of my childhood, for the following reason. My fifth-grade class at the Brooke Hill School for Girls, which was a lily-white private school in Birmingham, Alabama, had a big dinner party on the night of the local premiere. And the movie had opened about three months late in Birmingham in the spring of '63, reputedly because the content was so controversial that no theaters would show it. So the Birmingham Jaycees [Junior Chamber of Commerce] had a campaign to bring it to town, and it was this big deal. Our class dinner party was at the home of Studie and Walker Johnson, who were the twin daughters of the family that owned the Coca-Cola bottling franchise in Birmingham, and whenever we went to their house, we got to drink as many six-and-a-half-ounce bottles of Coke as we wanted. We had sort of fancy food; I recall there was sour cream in one of the dishes or something. And then seniors from our school drove us to the theater. The reason this was such a big party was that our classmate Mary Badham played Scout in the movie. So the first bit of cognitive dissonance I ran up against that evening was seeing Mary on the screen, because in the year between when she shot the movie and when she came to Brooke Hill in fifth grade, which was when I met her, she had hit puberty. The little Scout who looked seven years old in the movie was this gawky preteen.

Mary came from a kind of an eccentric family. They lived in this Addams Family–type house. Her mother was British and had dyed auburn hair. Her father was much older; he had been a general, and they were from a fairly old Birmingham family—to the extent that any family in Birmingham is old, since the city was founded in 1871! But anyway, it was fabulous seeing Mary up there, because she was so cute. And she got to roll down the street in that tire.

Every Southern child has an episode of cognitive dissonance having to do with race, when the beliefs that you've held are suddenly called into question. For a lot of Southern kids, the classic instance was when you got on the bus with your beloved "maid," as they were called, and then the bus driver reprimanded her or made her go to the back of the bus. For me, it was seeing *To Kill a Mockingbird*. I remember watching it, first assuming that Atticus was going to get Tom Robinson off, not only because Tom Robinson was innocent but because Atticus was played by Gregory Peck, and of course he was going to win. Then, as it dawned on me that it wasn't going to happen, I started getting upset about that. Then I started getting really upset about being upset, because by rooting for a black man you were kind of betraying every principle that you had been raised to believe in. And I remember thinking, *What would my father do if he saw me fighting back these tears when Tom Robinson gets shot?* It was a really disturbing experience. I'm sure that other girls in the theater that night were going through the same thing, but we never spoke of it at all.

We became obsessed with Scout. We started imitating Mary Badham and using her Scout expressions like "Cecil Jacobs is a big wet hen!" and "What the Sam Hill are you doing?" I remember asking my mother after seeing the movie, "What is Sam Hill?" There were all sorts of words I didn't understand, like *entailments* and *chiffarobe*. The one thing a lot of us memorized was the "Hey, Mr. Cunningham" speech, when Scout turns away the lynch mob in front of the jail. I look back on that as the little secret rite of passage we Brooke Hill girls shared, that we could cross over to the other side by identifying with turning away the lynch mob instead of being part of it, which was closer to where we were metaphorically in that time and place.

I think this may be one of those cases in which celebrity trumps controversy, because my mother, at least, was caught up in the whole Mary Badham phenomenon. The entire community was excited about her being nominated for an Academy Award for best supporting actress and annoyed when she lost to Patty Duke, who had played Helen Keller in *The Miracle Worker*. I certainly never talked to either of my parents about the content of the movie—and I barely even understood what rape was at the time. So it wasn't a parent-child talking opportunity at all.

But that experience summed up the whole school year to me. While researching my book nearly twenty years later, I was going through the local newspapers looking at the spring of '63, which was, of course, when Martin Luther King came to Birmingham and led the demonstrations that brought segregation to an end in America, with the fire hoses and police dogs attacking the children. I was scrolling through the newspapers, and I saw the movie ads for *To Kill a Mockingbird*, and I thought, *Wow, that's when that was?* Then I was reading the paper about the opening of the demonstrations in early April of 1963, and the very day that Project C, as King's campaign was called, began, there's an article saying something like "Klieg lights in Birmingham. Police ride up to the movie theater." It was about the premiere of this movie. I had never put those two together in my mind. What a perfect example of what C. Vann Woodward would call the irony of Southern history, that these two events should coincide.

My friends and I became addicted to the movie and would

go downtown every Saturday for matinees to see it again and to keep learning more speeches from it. Then one day our parents said, "You can't go downtown to the movies anymore." It was after the fire hoses and police dogs were turned against the young demonstrators. If you ask people my age in Birmingham, white people, what those demonstrations meant in their lives, they will, to a person, say, "Our parents would not let us go downtown to the movies anymore." And in my case, the movie that we were going downtown to see was *To Kill a Mockingbird*. The experience of watching the movie that first time was so traumatic, and I just remember trying to fight back those tears. I was the age that you don't want to cry in movies anyway, for anything. But to be crying for a black man was so taboo that I never forgot it.

I finally read the book in eighth grade, the year I was also reading a lot of those Daphne du Maurier and Mary Stewart books. I'd have these lost weekends of reading. I was just knocked out by it because I didn't think that the book would be even better than the movie. The voice-over in the movie is kind of straight and sincere—rather un-Scout-like, actually—but the narrative voice in the novel is salty and mischievous and hilarious. For example, I love the passage about Miss Maudie's reaction to a mere blade of nut grass in her yard, how she "likened such an occurrence unto an Old Testament pestilence." But it's funny, I don't have a specific memory of when I read the book, because it's one of those things that I feel has always been with me. I also don't remember hearing about the Sixteenth Street Baptist Church bombing, which was also one of those things that I felt was always in me.

There weren't that many people in Alabama to be proud of back then, and to be able to claim someone like Harper Lee was quite inspiring. We had Harper Lee from south Alabama;

we had Bear Bryant, the winning football coach; and then we had Wernher von Braun to the north in Huntsville, building the rocket that put us on the moon. Then again, von Braun was a transplant from Nazi Germany, so that left Harper Lee and Bear Bryant.

What are the odds of two people like Truman Capote and Nelle Harper Lee coming simultaneously out of a town like Monroeville? It's phenomenal, the incredible contrast between them: the one, who is considered the conscience of the country, and the other, who was probably a sociopath.

Most non-Southern readers would not understand how Atticus could stand up for Mrs. Dubose, because she was such a racist. Southerners understand this perfectly because the racism is kind of a given, especially in the time frame of the novel. One of the powerful and instructive things about the book is that even though it's such a classic indictment of racism, it's not really an indictment of the racist, because there's this recognition that those attitudes were "normal" then. For someone to rebel and stand up against them was exceptional, and Atticus doesn't take that much pride in doing so, just as he would have preferred not to have to be the one to shoot the mad dog. He simply does what he must do and doesn't make a big deal about it. Another skillful thing about the book is that Scout really does reflect the conditioning.

She does use the N word and still has that childlike befuddlement when she asks Calpurnia why she talks differently around her own people than she does around the Finches. Somebody now might find that too politically incorrect to put on the table. A lot of the novel is about what one is allowed to say, as in the morning after Scout averts the lynch mob, Atticus and Aunt Alexandra are arguing about whether he should have mentioned in front of Calpurnia that Mr. Underwood despises Negroes. It's interesting that she, the highly prejudiced one, is supposedly concerned about Calpurnia's "feelings." And in yet another layer of complexity, Mr. Underwood had been covering Atticus with his shotgun from his newspaper office the night before, siding with him against the mob—a little unsentimental coda to the scene that the movie left out. Harper Lee is willing and able to show without judgment what the conditions were like, partly because the action takes place in the past and partly because it's seen through the eyes of a child. But for a white person from the South to write a book like this in the late 1950s is really unusual—by its very existence an act of protest.

I think some of us have to leave the South to love it. You can't write about it if you don't love it, and it may be hard to love when you are down there amongst 'em.

Jon Meacham

Jon Meacham was born in Chattanooga, Tennessee, in 1969. He is the editor of Newsweek *and the author of three books, including* Franklin and Winston: An Intimate Portrait of an Epic Friendship *(2004) and* American Lion: Andrew Jackson in the White House, *which was awarded the Pulitzer Prize for biography in 2009.*

I first read *To Kill a Mockingbird* when I was in the eighth grade at McCallie School in Chattanooga, Tennessee, which is on Missionary Ridge, the old battlefield there. It was a small paperback, the kind if you got it all wet, it would be trouble. I remember very clearly reading it at home when I was about thirteen. The story was particularly appealing. I would have been Jem's age, more or less, and we knew that world of being outdoors all the time in the summer in the heat. It was not a foreign landscape to me: Boo Radley and the houses you didn't go to—I think every Southern neighborhood has that sort of mythology. Certainly ours did.

We all like to think that Atticus Finch was our father or our grandfather. They weren't, or it would have been a much better South, a much better country. There wouldn't have been the need for the novel if everyone had been like Atticus. He wasn't a caricature, either of good or of evil. And that's the way most folks were, and are. If you were a Southerner, you recognized almost everyone in *To Kill a Mockingbird*, and they weren't perfect. I think the courageous thing that Miss Lee did was end it on a tragic note. Melodrama would have ended with an acquittal. Instead it's a tale of good and evil that ends on a note of gray, which is where most of us live.

The ambiguity of the moral conclusion of the book became ever more real as I got older. I was with Harper Lee once in Sewanee, Tennessee, a couple of years ago at an occasion where Winston Churchill's daughter and Miss Lee were receiving honorary degrees from the University of the South. At one of the events, the recipient stands up and says how they got to be where they are, and when Harper Lee stood up, she simply looked at Churchill's daughter, Mary Soames, and said, "I would like to thank Lady Soames for everything, because if her father had not done what he did, I wouldn't have been able to write anything at all." And then she sat down. It was one of the most remarkably gracious things I have ever seen.

Telling it through Scout's eyes gives it a kind of Huckleberry Finn quality. Unlike some other narrators, Scout ages well—better, surely, than Holden Caulfield. For me, it evokes the kind of Southern courthouse world I grew up in, and the idea of paying tribute to a man even after he lost is quite moving and noble in many ways. Again, [I remember] being quite surprised even when very young that Atticus did not turn out to live happily after. I think the reason the book endures is it doesn't end on a fairy-tale note, and neither does life.

The fact that there has not been a second book is one of the great details in American literature: If you get it right once, stop.

Allison Moorer

Allison Moorer is a singer/songwriter whose ten albums include Mockingbird *(2008) and* Crows *(2010). She was born in Mobile, Alabama, in 1972. After her father killed her mother and himself in 1986, Moorer moved to Monroeville, Alabama, to live with relatives.*

I first read *To Kill a Mockingbird* when I was fifteen. I was in high school. It wasn't on our required summer reading list, even though I actually went to high school in Monroeville, Alabama, where Harper Lee lives, still, today. When I was a little kid, I remember seeing a copy of the book in my grandparents' house. And I always wondered about it, for some reason. I thought it was an interesting title, and I remember one of my older cousins was reading it.

I just reread it, and it's a very different book when you're an adult than it is when you're a kid—the significance of it in terms of justice, in terms of what's right and wrong, why people are the way they are, why people are racist, why people are bigoted. I am from the South; I live in New York part-time now. So reading about Southern people and Southern ways and the small-town South as someone who doesn't live there 365 days of the year anymore is interesting—to look at it from an outsider's point of view now.

What I see in the Southern small town is a lot of beauty, but I also see a lot of sadness. People are not small-minded because they want to be; they're small-minded because they have to be. I'm convinced that small-mindedness is a necessity for people who don't have an opportunity to be any other way. I don't believe that people want to be racist or homophobic, or whatever it is that they are. I think that it's a necessity for them to believe these things in order to function so their little worlds will hold together.

When I read the book, I saw what everybody who reads the book sees, that Tom Robinson was not guilty of what he was accused of. I didn't know how to wrap my head around what it really meant when I was fifteen and reading it at that time. I don't know if I do at this point grasp the notion of what it truly means to accuse someone of a crime they didn't commit.

I wanted to be Scout. I thought Scout was the coolest thing in the world. Obviously Scout's a very precocious child, and there were all kinds of things I liked about her. I liked that she could run and play with Jem and Dill. I liked her sense of humor and the whole Boo Radley subplot.

I didn't understand what the Boo Radley thing was about when I read it at fifteen. I didn't understand that Boo Radley is there as a character to represent our judgment of the things that we do not know. I definitely get that this time at the age of thirty-three.

Scout looked at the world through wide eyes rather than narrow ones. Her relationship with Calpurnia was really cool. I loved that she doesn't dig her aunt. When she says she could have sworn [Aunt Alexandra] was wearing that corset under her dressing gown, I thought she was exceptionally cool.

Monroeville is one of those typical old Southern towns built around the town square where the courthouse was. I haven't been to Monroeville in at least ten years. My aunt and uncle moved away, so I have no reason to go back there. There are quiet little streets. There was a black side of town, and there was a white side of town, and there still is. There's a little country club. It's just one of those little Southern towns that ['s] not going to get any bigger. It's going to get smaller. That's what happens to those towns.

The language really takes me back. This book was set in the thirties. My grandmother on my mother's side was born in 1926, so the way she talks is very much like the language in this book. The Southern way of speaking has changed quite a bit from that time. Even when I'm reading what Scout is thinking and what she's saying, I always put a soft *r* on it. That means instead of saying "close the door," it's "close the do-ah," like my grandmother says.

The Cunninghams: I remember being in school, being in first grade and noticing the kids who got free lunches, and I never had to have a free lunch, but I wondered at times why I didn't get free lunches, because we certainly didn't have any money. It was a pride thing. My parents weren't about to let me get free lunch at school, but there were parents who did, and I noticed. You know, kids do notice: that's one thing we forget. They take in everything.

The moment in the movie when somebody scares Dill and he turns around and says, "Good Lord, Aunt Stephanie, you like to scare me to death." I still say it, I do. That's what I say when I get scared. It's funny.

Harper Lee strikes me as a person who didn't ever want to put on airs, and that's another small-town activity she probably didn't want anything to do with. I get the feeling that people probably wanted to claim her in Monroeville early on, but they finally just gave up.

I wanted Atticus to be my dad. I wanted him to play with his kids. I loved who he was, and I loved that he was such a strong character and such a great dad to them. But I wanted him to have more fun.

I lost my mother at fourteen. So it was very fresh at that time. When I read it this year, I tuned into it in a different way. Kids who grow up without mothers—you can kind of spot 'em. They have a look or a way of being that's maybe a little different. Scout and Jem have Calpurnia, and lucky for them, because she obviously loved them and took an interest in them. But they're running around free. People looked out for them. I never see kids in trees anymore. I used to climb trees.

The thing about Scout that strikes me is she's so tough and so able to take care of herself. That toughness comes through in a way that I recognized. I grew up that way, feeling like I had to take care of myself and the rest of the world. I see that in Scout. She sort of has the world on her shoulders. That happens to kids that lose their parents. It happens to kids who have dysfunctional parents. In Scout you can feel her burden. She feels like she's got to figure it all out, or she's holding it all up. I definitely identified with that.

It's certainly none of my business—a person's art is their art—but I do find it fascinating that Harper Lee produced this amazing piece of work and that was it. And maybe that's all she had to say. Maybe that's it.

James Patterson

James Patterson was born in Newburgh, New York, in 1947. He is the author of more than fifty novels, including the Maximum Ride and Daniel X series for young readers. His Web site, Readkiddoread.com, is aimed at young reluctant readers. Patterson has sold more than 170 million books worldwide.

I read *To Kill a Mockingbird* in high school, and it was one of the few books I really liked. Part of my problem with going to this particular high school is they just didn't give us many books that would turn us on. My mother was a teacher, my father was an English major, but for some reason didn't bring books to me that might have turned me on as a reader as a kid. I was a good student, but I just didn't get turned on to reading. The two books I remember from high school that I did like a lot were *To Kill a Mockingbird* and *The Catcher in the Rye*—the usual, the staples. What I remember most about *To Kill a Mockingbird* was—and I think this probably is more of an American trait than in other places—I think we are particularly attuned to injustice. The stories that deal with injustice are really powerful here. I think we have more of a sense of that than they do in some places where injustice is more a fact of life. Here, much less so, for some people less so. So that really got to me. I loved the narration, how it went from a pleasant story to a quite horrifying one.

With both this book and *Huckleberry Finn*, it just got you thinking a lot about the way the world had changed, the way people think, and how they think so much differently now,

Sometimes people will criticize *To Kill a Mockingbird* because of certain language, but it expresses views of how people thought in the 1930s. Similarly people will write books about us now, and I am sure [in the future] people will be scandalized by the way we eat and the fact we're still having these ridiculous wars and whatever. But I think it's useful to kids, and it was useful to me to look back to an earlier time and see how different things were.

My connection was more to Jem, because he was a boy. I found the drama just kept building and building and building. In the beginning, you are suspecting something about Boo, which should tell you something about yourself, that you suspect him for no reason. It was a very, very emotional thing. The suspense was unusual in terms of books that I had read at that point, books that . . . had really powerful drama which really did hook you. Obviously, I try to do [that] with my books.

It was probably the first page-turner that I ever read, and yet it had greatness for a lot of reasons: the quality of the storytelling, the complexity of the story, the subject matter, the way it looked at a period with some compassion but also criticism of things going on.

Millions of kids in this country never read a book that they love. Part of the reason is they haven't been given a book they might fall in love with. I hope there would be more of an effort to mix it in school—more material that kids say, "I really liked *To Kill a Mockingbird*. It was cool." I cared about the characters. I thought about the book. I learned something.

I think *To Kill a Mockingbird* holds up because it's like an awful lot of classics, it's just good storytelling. It grabs your interest and it holds you. It keeps surprising you. Charles Dickens was a master at this. Whatever Harper Lee had on her mind, she must have realized that readers can get bored. When I write a story, I think I am telling a story to someone sitting across from me and I don't want them to get up. I would not like to have that happen, so I am always conscious of that. I would think that Harper Lee was also conscious of that. A lot of people might not stick with the story, and she wrote something that got you interested and kept surprising you.

One of the nice things about it was in the beginning it really puts you in touch with being a kid again. Books about childhood that do that are always irresistible to me. I'm always writing on my manuscripts, "Be there," which is to try to be there as a writer so the reader can be there. Even though not a lot happens the first summer with Dill, you're there and you are going along with the whole mini adventure. At this stage you have a feeling about Scout and Jem and Atticus, and then, oh my god, the building just crashes in, and the suspense kicks in [with] a little bit of what's going to happen to Tom Robinson, and this isn't fair, and especially as an American kid: This isn't fair, this isn't right. And when Jack, my eleven-year-old, read it, he had that same reaction: This isn't right. This isn't fair. This shouldn't happen.

Anna Quindlen

Anna Quindlen was born in Philadelphia in 1952. She is a Pulitzer Prize–winning columnist and the author of fifteen books, including the novels One True Thing *(1994)*, Rise and Shine *(2006), and* Every Last One *(2010). Her nonfiction books include* How Reading Changed My Life *(1998),* A Short Guide to a Happy Life *(2000), and* Good Dog. Stay. *(2007)*.

I took *To Kill a Mockingbird* out of the library at Holy Child Academy, where I went to school through eighth grade. But I can't exactly remember what year it was or how old I was.

I totally remember the experience. It's just all these people in this town, and you are visiting and you stay, and then at the end, you can't believe that you have to leave, and then sooner or later, you go back again and revisit them all over again. *To Kill a Mockingbird* is probably in the top three of books like that, where you utterly live in the book, and walk around in the book, and know everyone down to the ground in the book, and then leave, and then inevitably come back. I can't imagine anyone I like reading *To Kill a Mockingbird* and then not rereading it.

I've realized over the years that I have a completely different orientation toward the book than most people do, because at some essential level early on, and even as I got older, I don't really give a rip about Atticus. I mean, he is fine and he is a terrific dad and he does a wonderful thing, and so on and so forth.

But for me, this book is all about Scout. And I don't really care about anybody else in the book that much, except to the extent that they are nice to Scout and make life easier for Scout. I love Calpurnia because of Scout. I really like Jem and feel like I know him because of Scout. I'm totally perplexed by and sort of furious at Atticus when he has their aunt move in, who is just a heinous creature and is clearly there to get Scout to wear a skirt and wash her face, because I so don't want her to do anything like that. I think one of the reasons I became so obsessed with Harper Lee, when I was older and knew more about her biography, is because everything that she did convinced me that she was just a grown-up Scout who hadn't gone over to the dark side of being a girlie girl.

I looked over the book again about three months ago. It's still always about Scout to me because there really aren't that many of those girls. There were hardly any of those girls in our real life, and there aren't that many of them in books. So you store them up as a hedge against the attempts of the world to make you into something else.

Scout is totally real and totally imperfect, and she has the best two words in the book and two of the best words that have ever been put into any book by·any writer: "Hey, Boo." There are moments in books that make the hair stand up on the back of your neck, and "Hey, Boo" is one of those moments.

There are some women that you like, but they don't quite get the Scout thing. I remember being with a group of women once, talking about *Little Women* and asking about the characters, "Which one were you?" Every time someone would say Amy, my shoulders would sort of go up. And you do encounter that thing with *To Kill a Mockingbird* sometimes—people who just don't get Scout. I remember once someone telling me that they thought Scout was a peripheral character, and I was shocked out of my skin. They really thought Atticus was the centerpiece of the book, and it just isn't true.

There is that wonderful scene in the classroom where they have that new teacher who is very much the girlie girl, the one who tells her that Atticus taught her to read wrong and who then flips out because the cootie climbs out of the Ewell boy's hair. Scout just keeps trying to parse the world for this poor woman, to make her understand. She is much more like Atticus in some ways than Jem is, because you can tell there is this roving intelligence.

You can tell she is a writer, because she sees so much stuff. That moment when she is rolling down the hill in the tire and she hits the Radley house, and she hears the laugh from inside, but she sort of keeps it to herself for a long time. She can't even tell the people who are reading the book that she heard it. That is a writerly detail.

I feel like a lightning bolt is going to come through the ceiling, but I have to say that *To Kill a Mockingbird* isn't a writerly book. There are not a whole lot of verbal pyrotechnics. It's not a Southern novel in that way. When we think of the classic southern novels, we think of Faulkner, for example: detail upon detail and metaphor upon metaphor. This is a pretty plainly told story. It reminds you of that old saw that editors tell reporters: If you've got a story to tell, tell it; if you don't have a story to tell, write it. She's got a story to tell, so she doesn't have to use verbal pyrotechnics. There are some small moments when she lets the writing bring the way the street looks or the town looks into sharper focus. But just look at the way, for example, she describes the ham costume, which has always been, to me, kind of a Rosetta Stone. Scout isn't dressed up like Bo Peep or an antebellum Southern girl. She is dressed like a ham, and the description is as basic as can be. [Mrs. Crenshaw, the local seamstress] molds chicken wire, puts canvas over it, and paints it. The fact is, you totally get it. You can see that ham in your mind's eye. So she does not make the writing do the work. She lets the story do the work. One of the interesting things is, for example, that the prose could not be more different than Capote's prose, which is so fulsome that sometimes when you are reading *Other Voices, Other Rooms*, you think, *Oh please! Just pull back 20 percent for me.* She has pulled all the way back to the bare bones of story and character—mainly character, I think.

I don't think Truman Capote had anything to do with *To Kill a Mockingbird*. Come on, think of how he would have ginned up all kinds of scenes in that book. There is just no way, to my way of thinking. You know, just by reading *To Kill a Mockingbird*, that Harper Lee, who is obviously Scout, is a person with a grounded self-esteem, surrounded by affection. Whereas you have that horrible moment where her hideous second cousin, Francis, the one that she beats up and calls a whore-lady with no idea what that means, says something terrible about Dill, who is based on the boy Truman Capote. He says he doesn't come to visit in the summer. His mother doesn't want him and she passes him around from person to person, and you think, *Oh, that little boy is going to be in real trouble*, and, of course, that little boy was.

There is a trancelike aspect to the whole thing. Those people become more real than real people are. It's what you are aiming for when you're writing a novel, that you'll feel like the characters are more real than the people you eat dinner with every night. And the other thing that is so incredibly engaging about it is that it feels true. Sometimes people will say, "Well, I don't like the ending to this book or that book because it makes me sad or it wasn't satisfactory." In this book, you know where it's going to end, because you know what the true thing would be to have happened. The way things play out in the courtroom and then the way things play out that night when Scout is walking home in the ham costume, which is incredibly terrifying, and then the resolution of the Radley story, which is about as affecting as any story line that you can imagine. Every kid has had that house in the neighborhood that your friends would dare you to knock at on Halloween. The idea that the person in that house is not a monster but a prisoner is so beautifully wrought in this book that I think you're just totally present in it the whole time you are reading it. At that moment when she says "Hey, Boo" and her father says, "Jean Louise, this is Mr. Arthur Radley"—it doesn't get any better than that.

This book is filled with the use of the word *nigger*. I mean, it is in here over and over again, and somehow, it stays off the banned book list. [*To Kill a Mockingbird* is often challenged, however. It is number 23 on the American Library Association's list of the 100 Most Frequently Challenged Books.] I haven't seen the kind of uproar [as for *Huckleberry Finn*], and I think it is because the relationship between the white people and the black people in the book is so true, not to the understanding of white people, but to the understanding of black people. There is nothing condescending about it. There is that moment when Calpurnia takes them to church and people are saying they have their own church, don't bring them to our church, and Calpurnia says, well, you know, I'm taking care of them, or they are my children, or something like that, and one of the women says, is that what you call what you do during the week? To make clear: OK, we all know there is a pecking order here, and language is harsh, and the way they characterize each other is harsh, but the truth surmounts the harshness, in a way. It doesn't blunt it. It justifies it.

I think there are certain books in which the characters are so real and so vivid that you feel as though they've become close personal friends. And that goes a long way to explaining why books last.

That's the reason why *A Tree Grows in Brooklyn*, which in many ways could feel quite antiquated, still sells every year, because Francie is somebody that readers feel as though they know, and so they revisit her over and over again.

I think there is no question that that's true of this book. It is also a tremendous teaching tool. If I were teaching eighth graders and I wanted to talk about prejudice and doing the right thing and doing the hard thing and what it means to be female and what it means to be a citizen, this is on the top three or four. So it keeps coming around again in that way. And I think there are also books that give you a feeling about your possible best self, and this is one of those books. *A Wrinkle in Time* is one of those books. *Little Women* is one of those books, and this is definitely one of those books. That sense of being part of something that calls upon the best that people can be—that's really exciting and satisfying, and that gets you in the gut.

People tend to dismiss books in which the centerpieces are children or young adults. I think it is very easy to slot this into the Young Adult category like some of the other books that I've mentioned. I just think that's stupid. You can call *The Catcher in the Rye* a young-adult novel all you want, but it's still going to speak to this new generation of readers.

The difference between *The Catcher in the Rye* and *To Kill a Mockingbird* is, *The Catcher in the Rye* usually doesn't survive adulthood. I've known some people who've gone back and read it and thought, *This was my favorite book when I was sixteen. What was I thinking?* I don't know anybody who feels that way about *To Kill a Mockingbird*. You come back to it and you are still just sucked right into it. You know, you are sucked into it in a completely different way as an adult than you were as a kid because you understand what Atticus is facing as what was not then called the single parent. You are sucked right back in it. By the way, in his own times, Dickens's work was denigrated all the time because it was popular. I love the literary tradition that suggests that if something is popular, it can't really be first-rate. Give me a break.

I know a fair amount about Harper Lee. Every year or two, when I was a young reporter, I used to put in a formal request to interview Harper Lee. As a writer, there were a couple of things that obsessed me about her. There are lots of writers who have one great book in them; most of them write seven or eight. I was drawn to the notion of a woman who wrote one great book and then packed it in, for whatever reason. There are different theories about why she did so, but I loved that idea. The second thing was that as someone who has been on both sides of the yawning maw of the publicity machine, who has both interviewed countless authors and been interviewed many, many times, I love the fact that she wouldn't play. Every time I got turned down for an interview, there was part of me that thought, *Oh yeah!* I gathered that HarperCollins had a very polite nice boilerplate letter that they sent to hundreds or thousands of us over the years, and I got it a couple of times.

Look—a million times, I've been asked with each of my books, "Are you going to write a sequel to *Black and Blue*? Are you going to write a sequel to *Blessings*?" Can you imagine the pressure on Harper Lee to write a sequel to *To Kill a Mockingbird* once the movie came out and you could see that it kept selling every year? They just must have thrown rose petals and chocolates and millions of dollars at her feet, and I don't know whether she couldn't do it, but I prefer to think she wouldn't do it because, of course, it's utterly wrong.

Richard Russo

Richard Russo was born in Johnstown, New York, in 1949. He is the author of seven novels, including Mohawk (1986); Nobody's Fool (1993); Empire Falls (2002), winner of the Pulitzer Prize for fiction; and That Old Cape Magic (2009). He is a screenwriter and retired professor.

*T*he first time I read *To Kill a Mockingbird*, I don't think I finished it, and the reason I didn't finish it was that at the time I would have been in high school. And at that time, I had what was a hard-and-fast rule, which was to read everything I could get my hands on except what was assigned to me. It was Catholic school, and I was in that rebellious frame of mind that if somebody else wanted me to read it, it was probably crap.

So I went into *To Kill a Mockingbird* with that notion that it was like the other books that the nuns wanted me to read. So I remember reading and reluctantly thinking, *This is really good*, but I couldn't admit to it. I couldn't admit it to them; I couldn't admit it to myself.

There was that father/daughter relationship, which burrowed under my skin even then. Those of us who become writers are becoming writers long before we ever put pen to paper. In *Great Expectations*, which I didn't finish either, because it too had been assigned, there was something about the opening scenes of that book where Pip and Magwitch come together. There was something that burrowed into me there—a way in which you can be ashamed of someone you love, the way Joe Gargery is. That relationship between Joe Gargery and Pip really burrowed underneath, because I had a father who was largely absent, and when he came back, it was a small town and everybody wanted to know why my father didn't live with us. So there was something about the opening of *Great Expectations* that burrowed very, very deep.

To Kill a Mockingbird was that way, even though I didn't finish the book, even though I was stubbornly a teenager. In some way it probably frightened me, something about that book frightened me. I look back on it now in the way in which you are becoming a writer and certain books influence you. It's hard to imagine *Empire Falls* being written without *To Kill a Mockingbird*, because I don't think Tick could have existed without Scout—something about that father/daughter relationship. When I came back to it as an adult, a lot of the way I felt about my daughters and the way in which they were going about in the world, the way Scout does, is there.

Scout loves her father, but the truth is, young people are to a certain extent on their own, and they're learning about life through their own eyes and own experiences.

And in the best father/daughter relationship there are going to be huge areas of their lives that you don't have access to, you're not privy to; you weren't there. And a lot of people always ask me, "Why did you give that beautiful child in your novel the name of an ugly bug?" I always tell them, "I wanted a name as memorable for this character in my book as Scout is memorable in *To Kill a Mockingbird*."

I went back and read it and, of course, recognized it for the masterpiece that it was. And it aided me in writing all of my father/daughter stuff, all my family stuff, because that is a quintessential American family, even though it's not typical.

Atticus Finch, in some ways, was the father maybe that I longed for. But when I became a father, I found it very difficult to be that kind of father. I have found it impossible not to tell my daughters how much I love them at every juncture. Atticus is reserved. He trusts his daughter. He trusts his daughter to understand what is essential about him and about herself and about their relationship. I could never have gone about it that way, and yet there was some part of me that knew as a father that less would have been more. I think Atticus knew that and was able to act upon it as a principle. That great ability to trust a child and that great ability to understand that a child will know in the fullness of time what it is that you're trying to get across.

And that what you do, even more than what you say, will be all that that child ultimately will need. I didn't have that great faith he seems to have in that book.

Back when I was teaching, I used to remind my students that masterpieces are masterpieces not because they are flawless but because they've tapped into something essential to us, at the heart of who we are and how we live.

Writing, it seems to me, is often taught, from the time that we're in grade school, as the absence of mistakes—when you get your first papers back, and you have a little X that's an error, another X that's an error. Right up through college, I remember being taught that way, that careless errors, the difference between T-H-E-I-R and T-H-E-R-E—you get counted off for that.

And so every time you get a little check, then, you have lost points. And I lost points. But somehow you never *gained* points. You started off with a hundred points, and then for every mistake that you made, you lost points. If you're trying to teach fiction writing or any kind of decent writing, any kind of real writing to students, the first thing you have to do is get them out of that frame of mind whereby you lose points for mistakes.

I think *To Kill a Mockingbird* is like *Moby-Dick*, in a sense; it's not like you can't find things wrong with it. When I read it as an adult, I remember thinking there were passages of exposition that I would have done differently. Or there were passages that were maybe a little bit clunky in terms of its style, although parts of it are just incredibly graceful, wonderfully graceful.

Great books are not flawless books. Look at the ending to *Huckleberry Finn*, maybe the great American novel—it is a huge misstep. You cannot imagine Twain taking them on that journey down the Mississippi and then somehow reverting into *Tom Sawyer* land at the end. It's a betrayal of everything that he had done earlier in the book. It's a flaw, but so what? The thing about writing is, you're not looking for an absence of errors. You're not looking for a pristine slate. You're not looking for things to be perfect, but something has to hit you where you live.

There's one of those columns in *Newsweek* or *Time*—a writer talks about five books that were tremendously important, and then, What's a book that you've reread that didn't stand up? And someone, I can't remember who, named *To Kill a Mockingbird*, and I remember thinking, *Whoa, maybe you need to read it again.* Because that book holds up the way great books do. They just touch you in that very deep place.

For me it had something to do with that father/daughter relationship. It had something to do with a time when we really believed in justice—the necessity of justice as a part of our lives, the possibility of trying to make a just world. All of that was incredibly powerful. I think it's an indispensable book.

Whenever a writer is gifted enough and fortunate enough to write a book as good as that, you can't help but think, *What else?* Maybe that's the fallacy. Maybe it's a fallacy to think that if you could write a book that good, you must have had seven or eight others in you just like it.

There's a line of logic that suggests, if you can do it once, then maybe you can do it again or again and again and again. Dickens wrote one novel, one great novel right after another. I know when I read a book like *To Kill a Mockingbird* and realize there's only one, I feel a deep sinking feeling as a result of that. The one was a gift and you'd be pretty careless to say you deserve more. But some part of you does think, *Why not more?*

When somebody writes *To Kill a Mockingbird*, you just hope they're happy.

Lizzie Skurnick

Lizzie Skurnick was born in New York in 1973. She is the author of Shelf Discovery: The Teen Classics We Never Stopped Reading *(2009) and is the Fine Lines columnist for Jezebel.com, where she writes about young-adult classics. A contributor to NPR, the* New York Times, *and the* Daily Beast, *she has written books for three young-adult series, Sweet Valley, Love Stories, and Alias.*

I read *To Kill a Mockingbird* in class. I remember the edition. It was the yellow paperback with no illustration on the cover, just *To Kill a Mockingbird* in big block type and "Harper Lee." I think it was probably the first novel that I ever read that fully inhabited a girl's consciousness in a very immediate and complicated way.

I thought Scout was a boy for a page and a half. I was a very fast reader, and I wasn't paying attention at some key part. I remember being thrilled when I realized it was a girl, but also very surprised, because I hadn't read a lot of novels with girl protagonists who weren't in hoop skirts and riding out West. I didn't know the Southern girl tomboy. I didn't really understand that genre of a prepubescent girl—and the novel is not about her growing sexuality, so that was also a new thing to me.

I think it took me awhile to really locate what kind of a character Scout was, because she is also a "character" in the best sense of the word. Generally speaking, a young girl in such circumstances is sort of spunky or someone you're supposed to side with, someone who is going to have interesting adventures.

Scout is all those things, but it's a dark, lonely novel from the beginning, in its own way. Scout is not a happy girl setting off on the prairie. Her life is very complex. She doesn't have a mother. Her father is an interesting man, but he's not like Pa in *Little House on the Prairie*. He doesn't set her on his knee and play the violin all night, he doesn't buy them tin cups and put pennies in them.

In many ways, her childhood is very lonely, and it's only her interest in other people that makes it a full childhood. She's really an explorer, but I don't think the exploration is cast in any way that makes it seem fun or endearing. You get the sense it's really how one might be as an adult, put into a foreign city, forced to create a life for oneself.

You're not supposed to feel sorry for Scout. I never felt sorry for her. It's only that when you go back and look at it as an adult that you see you might as well be reading *Ethan Frome*. It's a sad novel in a lot of ways.

As a girl, I was never even interested in the court case. I felt like that was an explicit plot really put in for the adults. I know that's the whole point of this novel: that it's about the South, that it's about justice, that it's about how life doesn't work out OK. But I feel that that's something established within the first chapter. I didn't need her to learn any lesson for it to become interesting for me.

In some ways, I think, for me, that's the weakest part of the novel. It's the lesson for the reader, really.

Going back and looking at the novels of the period of the sixties, seventies, and eighties, I've often noted that the girls are filled with a lot of anger. They're difficult girls. They're not necessarily the child you'd want to babysit. In fact, they're definitely not the child you'd want to babysit. There's nothing charming about them at all.

So that's who Scout makes me think of. And in some ways, she makes me think of Laura [in *Little House on the Prairie*], although Laura is her precursor. I've always thought that Laura is interesting to girls. The reason why those Laura Ingalls Wilder novels are not about Mary [Laura's sister] is that Mary is so boring. She's got no conflict. She doesn't struggle with life. Laura really is always trying to control herself and to make sure she doesn't damage what she loves.

I think that's true of Scout, too. She struggles with things in a very genuine way. She's always having to ask for forgiveness or figure things out or repair things that she's done, but she's not a bad girl.

She truly struggles in the way we struggle as adults to figure out how to be in the world.

The second half of the novel, those grand themes of justice, injustice—those are about how the world acts on us. But Scout is really about who we are in the world, how we decide that.

Scout maybe doesn't understand that she's a seeker. Scout is maybe a little too young to feel justified in her curiosity about the world, especially when there are very few happy answers to the things she's curious about.

I think they were teaching it to us with this idea of children can be exposed to the adult world, and here's what happens when children are exposed to it: They learn. And I really felt Scout was interesting on her own. I don't think she needed that case to become interesting.

Lee Smith

Lee Smith was born in 1944 in Grundy, Virginia. A retired professor, she is the author of twelve novels, including The Last Girls *(2002) and* On Agate Hill *(2008), and a short-story collection,* Mrs. Darcy and the Blue-Eyed Stranger *(2010).*

*T*he first time I read *To Kill a Mockingbird*, I was in high school and I was just knocked out. I was especially fascinated because I was from the mountain South, where we had no black people. We had our own sort of weird class system of who lived in the town and who lived in the hollers. But the novel was about a whole different South, and it was just incredible to me.

It made me think a lot about the poorer people among us, the marginalized people in the Appalachian South who were discriminated against in so many ways. You can't really romanticize racism, but picturesque poor people on their porches chewing tobacco and stuff, you can.

So *To Kill a Mockingbird* brought me a whole new awareness of people who were *other*, and what they suffered because of it. It is fair to say that this novel changed my life—changed the way I thought about race, class, and discrimination.

Another experience that I had with this book was between my junior and senior year in college, the summer of '66. I was working for a newspaper in Richmond, Virginia, and Hanover County had just banned *To Kill a Mockingbird* then. [When a prominent physician protested that a novel with rape in its plot was "improper for our children to read," the Hanover County school board ordered all copies of *To Kill a Mockingbird* off the shelves, calling it "immoral literature."] The editor of the newspaper said that any child who wanted a copy of *To Kill a Mockingbird* should write him a personal letter and tell him why, and we would send them one. Well, I was the one who sent 'em. I thought I was going to be a star reporter, of course, and basically all I did was address copies of *To Kill a Mockingbird* and send them out to every child in Hanover County. I thought it was fabulous, though. I was proud to be doing this.

I think one of the amazing things about the writing in *To Kill a Mockingbird* is the economy with which Harper Lee delineates not only race—white and black within a small community—but class. I mean *different kinds* of black people and white people both, from poor white trash to the upper crust—the whole social fabric.

I have taught *To Kill a Mockingbird* for years, from junior high to graduate school; I have read it probably twenty-some-odd times. And every single time, it rewards you, and you see something new. I think at first the thing that strikes you so strongly is the depiction of racism and the tragedy of race. But Boo Radley is indelible too. Boo Radley cannot be overestimated as an important factor in this book because every neighborhood has that house that's overgrown and those neighbors that are weird or that you never ever, ever see. And stories grow up about them. I think that figure always occupies a place in a child's imagination. And to demystify that—to make us see that people so radically different from us are OK, and can be helpful and wonderful—I think this is so important.

There is no more dramatic book, when you think about the pacing and the order of chapters and the way Boo Radley keeps coming back and coming back, and then the Ewells sneaking around. It is an incredibly dramatic book.

The novel is also dead-on about childhood; it evokes childhood so beautifully. But it also evokes the whole community. I think we forget sometimes that kids live *in community*, and it's so helpful in terms of how children relate to older people in the community. There's also something so evocative about the fact that these are motherless children, although they do have Calpurnia, and they do have their aunt. Somehow, I think, all children, in a way, feel isolated—nobody feels the things that they feel. Because these are motherless children, I think the young reader empathizes with Scout and Jem even that much more; Dill too, who doesn't get along with his stepfather. So they're kids against the world—I think that's very attractive to younger readers.

When I was growing up, girls in the South were—and are still today, I think—oftentimes raised to be fitting into some sort of a ladylike mold where they are not supposed to express feelings and they are not supposed to stand up for things. I just think of girls in the South being squashed as they're being raised. So the role that Scout has played in all these girls' minds as they have read the book is very important. Here's Scout who believes in things, who is funny and curious and passionate and a tomboy. I think Scout has done more for Southern womanhood than any other character in literature. I'm quite serious. She's turned girls into the kind of women we want.

I think one thing that is really important to remember is that students are reading it today with the same responses we all had in the sixties. I just spent a day in a high school doing a workshop, and it was funny, at first I could not get the students to talk to me about what they were reading. Then a boy said *To Kill a Mockingbird*, and everybody started talking about it and what they had gotten out if it—every single one of them! It still has a galvanizing effect on a younger reader.

This is a novel which *endures*, as opposed to other classics which don't appeal as much to readers today. *The Sun Also Rises* is a good example, because students just say, "Who are all these people drinking in Spain? What is this about?" You never get that reaction to *To Kill a Mockingbird*. It remains as relevant today as it was the day it was written. It never ages. It's a story of maturing, certainly, and initiation, but told in such beautifully specific terms that it never seems generic.

People want to read something with real substance. I think

they want to read a novel that gives us all something to believe in. And I think *To Kill a Mockingbird* manages to do that without being too preachy.

Most writers write entirely too much, 'cause it's what we love, it's our passion. And I know it's Harper Lee's passion too, because nobody can write like this who doesn't feel like that. So I absolutely don't understand why we don't have another book. Maybe there will be a great number of them left for us sometime. I don't see how she could bear not to be writing, with a talent like this.

Lots of times I've had trouble writing, but I've always felt a need to do it, because it's the way I've made sense of my life. I think that's true for most of us. It's just astonishing to me that Harper Lee just stopped. I bet she hasn't, I bet she's sneaking around doing it. I bet she's sitting in her house like Boo Radley, writing. I hope so.

Adriana Trigiani

Adriana Trigiani grew up in Big Stone Gap, Virginia, in the 1970s. She is a documentary filmmaker, playwright, and television writer/producer.

She has written ten novels, including Big Stone Gap (2001), Lucia, Lucia (2004), and Very Valentine (2009). In 2009, Trigiani published the first in a series of books for young adults: Viola in Reel Life.

I got *To Kill a Mockingbird* off of the Wise County Bookmobile in Big Stone Gap, Virginia. And I was twelve years old. It was a perfect time to read it, because around that age I became aware of the different backgrounds of people in the community. I was hyperaware of ethnic differences, because we were Italians in a small Southern town, so we felt like we were from Pluto. This book really helped me understand how segregated the South was before we arrived. 'Cause I really didn't get it. I didn't know the South before integration.

It's interesting that I chose the book at all, because the title *To Kill a Mockingbird* is very literary. As a child, I found the title off-putting, because I was reading *Harriet the Spy* by Louise Fitzhugh at that time.

At first, I thought Harper Lee could be a man, it sounded like a man's name to me. Then I found out Harper Lee was a woman author. And I was thrilled. Harper Lee seemed to embody the character of Scout. You felt that, in this instance, the author was the character. *To Kill a Mockingbird* hooked me on books written in the first person. I wanted the author to speak directly to me. I love the voice of the first person, whether it's *To Kill a Mockingbird* or *Jane Eyre*. When the author writes in the first person, I feel like I know her by the end. And you sure feel like you know Scout by the end of this novel.

To Kill a Mockingbird is really the model for anyone who wants to write a story in the first person. Harper Lee writes with humor and such grace that as a reader, you're sold the minute you read the first sentence. You're with her for the journey of this book and this story.

Harper Lee takes you inside a character, and then she takes you outside the character, and then she takes you back in again. She lets you know, in really gorgeous prose, what the character is feeling and also how everyone around her feels about her. This is really hard to do. There's that old John Ruskin quote about writers who must learn to tell what they see "in a plain way." Imagine that scene with Aunt Alexandra with the Add-A-Pearl necklace and the dresses and how a girl is supposed to behave. And how Scout stands up for herself with common sense and says, in effect, Well, I can do that in pants. Scout is just a fantastic character, written with such an authentic voice and such honesty.

People are always bemoaning the fact that Harper Lee never wrote another novel, but I think it's great that this novel was her definitive work. If you're going to write a book, write one of the great American classics and say what you need to say. When an author writes a lot of novels, I think we're simply turning the same rock over and over again, exploring the same themes, solving the same riddle. We're just dealing with the same issues over and over again. And if you feel that you've completed that mission and that you've written about it the best you can, really, what else is there to say? I think it's great that *To Kill a Mockingbird* is Harper Lee's opus and that we can read [it] time and time again.

Also, I think, to a great degree, the craft of writing novels in order to sell them has changed. It used to be that a novelist would write a book and you got to have that glorious life of solitude and quietude. You could just stay in your room and do your work. After all, we become writers because we like to be by ourselves and create, figure things out. Now, after we write a book, it's incumbent upon us to go on the road and sell it. We have to be with the public.

Now, there are great, wonderful things about that that I wouldn't trade for anything. I like to talk with my readers. But for some authors, it really defeats the purpose of being a writer. Some authors don't want to be out and about, milling around talking to people. I think Harper Lee's quest for solitude and quietude is really admirable in a time when everyone's required to be out on the street with a sandwich board, selling their work. Once the publishing houses knew that you could reach a wider audience by traveling to your readers, they sent you out. After all, it's a business.

For Harper Lee, her novel rolled out beautifully, it sold beautifully, it took on a life of its own, and its success had very little to do with the fact that she had to be out selling it. The book stood for itself. It would be nice to have that kind of a culture today, but we don't anymore. The world is big and yet tiny, because we have access to anybody at any time, any place through e-mail, telephone—whatever. It's a different time, and I think how delicious it must have been to be Harper Lee when *To Kill a Mockingbird* came out. She was home and would receive these handwritten letters. For that to be your main source of communication with your public was so great. She could sit down and answer those letters at her leisure or just savor them and not answer them at all. She could do whatever she wanted to do.

Good for her. Good for Harper Lee, for being the person she is, knowing her limitations, knowing what she wanted to do, knowing when to quit, and knowing when to say, "Enough." Imagine actually knowing when enough is enough. Maybe she felt that this novel said it all. Any reader will tell you that she accomplished her goal.

I think this book speaks to kids today because of the nontraditional settings children are being raised in. Blended families didn't exist then to the degree that they do now. I was in this big Italian family, and I craved the kind of life [Scout] had. She seemed to me to be fiercely independent; there seemed to be a streak of Pippi Longstocking in her, like she owned the town, and that appealed to me.

Atticus Finch, a decent man, a man of principle and values, was a model to Scout. He gave Scout a sense of self-esteem, of self-confidence. Her ideas were not put down. She was heard. And yet everyone does not treat her as Atticus does. Aunt Alexandra puts pressure on Scout, on the way [Scout] looks. Well, this is what we do to girls in life. We imply, *You're worth something if you're beautiful. You're worth something if you're appealing. You're not, really, if you aren't.*

What I always loved about Atticus was that he had common sense and a clean, clear notion for his daughter, Scout: Be who you are. And that's enough, and by the way, that's pretty great. A child needs to hear that, whether it comes from a parent or a parental figure, an aunt or uncle, whoever it happens to be. So I thought their relationship was beautiful and profound, and when I read it the first time, it felt right and comfortable to me. *Yeah,* I thought. *You're a great girl. Be who you are.*

My father died in 2002. I find it incredibly difficult to write his voice. Harper Lee wrote her father's voice. And she not only wrote her father's voice, she nailed his temperament, his appearance, his place in the community, his ability in the courtroom, his professional life. It's as if she had an insight into him that no one else did, which is another reason why this book is so compelling. Harper Lee was able to take complex, grown-up issues and really bring them down to their root basics, so that the reader could understand and embrace the characters and the story. She did it perfectly. That would be another reason never to write another book. When you get that right, your hunt is done. You're finished, in a certain way.

Also, if you write about the person who you feel was instrumental in your life in an honest way, you've said all there is to say. Artistic process is so much about formulating, Why was I put in this family and where do I fit in it, and why did I get these parents? And once you get past the why, which is some kind of mystical thing, and you attempt to communicate those relationships as a writer, that's the tough stuff, the bare-bones work. Our job is to describe people and to remember how they sounded, and then to relay that to a reader. Harper Lee studied her father, observed everything about him, enough to explain him to us, her readers.

You know, my father used to say, "Don't do as I do, do as I say." But if you really want to understand someone, watch what they do. Actions define character. As a parent, when I reread *To Kill a Mockingbird* today, I think, *Wow, there's really an important message in here for parents. You think that you're watching your kids 24/7. But they're really watching you.*

Art is the emotional landscape of a culture. It's our feelings talking, in whatever form it is, whether it's a dance, a poem, a short story, a novel. *To Kill a Mockingbird* is the best of American literature because it tells us who we are, who we can be, and it paints the communities we lived in, in vivid, truthful detail. I mean, if that's not art, or our highest dreams for literature, for storytelling, I don't know what is.

Mary Tucker

Mary Tucker was born in Burnt Corn, Alabama, in 1927. She has lived in Monroeville, Alabama, since 1954 and taught in its public schools before and after integration.

I moved to Monroeville in 1954 after marrying John Tucker, who lived in Monroeville. The town, as all the Southern towns were at that time, was segregated. There had been quite a bit of development from the time of *To Kill a Mockingbird*, set in the 1930s. The streets were all paved around the square and into town. It was very segregated. We could not use the restaurants in town. The library was segregated. Churches were very segregated. I was taking a correspondence course on the short story. And there were several books that we didn't have in our school library nor in the little branch library in the black community. So I went to the library in town. Mrs. Mort McMillan was the librarian, and I told her what I needed and asked if she would borrow the books through the interlibrary loan. She agreed, and I would pick the books up and take them home and use them. I didn't try to use them in the library. But she was very nice about getting the books that I needed.

When I first came to Monroeville, I lived outside of the city limits, the place where my husband grew up. And then we built a house in town in 1960 on Drury Road. The area where I lived was called the Morning Star community, which was practically all black, but on the street right behind me was a white area. And then the other black community was down in what is called Clausel, where the black high school was, Union High School.

Downtown was all white. There were some homes right outside of the business area, but that was all white. There were no black businesses at all in downtown. The closest was a cleaners at that time; it was New Modern, which was owned by a black man. I can't remember the year that the first black policeman was hired, but it must have been in the late seventies. Vanity Fair [the lingerie company] was very segregated. They did not hire any blacks except as truck drivers and janitors until they were forced to in the seventies, I believe. And one lady who was hired there told me that her supervisor told her, "We had to hire you. We didn't want to."

When I came to Monroeville, at one of the little dress shops, I was told that if I tried on a dress, it had to be over the clothes that I was wearing, [unlike white customers], which surprised me. I resented that I couldn't use the library. We would go to the drugstore, where they had a soda shop, and I couldn't sit down and have a Coke or ice cream. I resented those things. I taught in Beatrice when I first came to Monroe County, from 1957 till 1960. And then I taught at Union High until schools integrated.

I resented the fact that our black students from the lower part of the county would come to Union High School and drive past Monroe County High. And they were often late, and they left early to get home before dark. So, yes, I resented that.

And I knew we didn't have the equipment that they had at Monroe County High School.

Black people stayed in their neighborhoods, so I didn't really notice any tension. We shopped in town, but other than that, we didn't have any interaction with whites. We were just very separate. I didn't know any white people except the businesspeople that I had dealings with, and the professionals. My doctor, Dr. Rayford Smith, was great, but I had no interaction with whites.

Integration actually went well in Monroeville. I think the student body and the public schools were about 45 percent white and 55 percent black, but it went extremely well. My husband was the principal of the middle school. He had great support from some of the leaders in the white community. Many have told me that they think that he was one of the reasons that it went so well.

After integration, I've just gotten to know many more of the whites. I have attended community Bible study up at First Baptist, where I met a lot of people. And then I've served on various boards—the library board, the museum board, and now the historic preservation board—where I have gotten to know and had interactions with many whites.

There certainly was some progressive thinking in town, but they could not go against the conventions. Before integration, A. B. Blass [owner of the hardware store] used to tell a story about the Christmas parade that was sponsored by the Kiwanis Club, I believe. This was in the sixties before schools integrated. A white citizens council had been organized, and the Klan was still active. And A.B. said that he was told that if the black band from Union High School marched in the parade, there would be trouble. Mr. McMillan, the principal, was told that the high school black band was not to march.

And so, rather than not permit our band to march, they canceled the parade. A.B. ran a hardware store, and he said that his business suffered because of his decision. So we didn't have the Christmas parade that year.

There was the civil rights movement, but we didn't have much activity in Monroeville. There was in the county just north of us, Wilcox, but not very much in Monroeville. I was told by one of the civil rights activists, Ezra Cunningham from Beatrice, that he tried to get blacks registered to vote. Now, I had no trouble registering. When I went up, the only thing that bothered me, the registrars insisted on filling out the form for me.

I registered soon after I came, so it must have been '55. But

Mr. Cunningham told me he reached an agreement with the town officials that he would just bring five people per week. So they didn't feel threatened. And those five people were able to register to vote.

He said there were repercussions. He was told one time that if he came to Monroeville on a certain route, there would be people waiting for him. And the Board of Education threatened to send his wife over to Lower Peachtree, which is quite a distance away, when she was teaching at her home in Beatrice. So he said that he suffered repercussions and that he couldn't get a car loan.

I read the book as soon as it came out and I got my hands on it. I loved it. I was very much impressed. I knew Miss Alice Lee, because when we got a loan to build our house, she was our lawyer. I didn't know that many people in the white community; I didn't know their reaction to the book until much later. Not a lot of black people read the book. Later on, I discovered that many did not like it, still don't. Some have told me they don't see the play because they don't like the language. And I've tried to explain that the use of the N word was a part of the vocabulary of that time. If they had changed it, it wouldn't have been realistic. But some still don't appreciate the book. I'm talking about the black population. They are the ones that don't like the language.

White people in town thought that many of the characters were really based on real people. And I understand they resented that. And Atticus's defense of a black man, I heard, much later; I really didn't know their thinking then, but I've heard, much later. And from what one of my white neighbors told me, that she hated that book, the way they treated the Boulware boy, she said.

Boo Radley: My husband told me he remembered the incident, that he was one of the teenagers who got into some trouble, and his father, rather than allow him to be incarcerated, said he would lock him up at home and that he would never get in trouble again. My husband remembered that incident.

The church that's mentioned, where Calpunia brought the children, because that was in easy walking distance—I think that was my church, Morning Star. I remember [my husband's] aunt telling me of her father, who was white, who lived outside of town, bringing them into town to shop. And they didn't want to be seen coming into town with a white man, who was their father. They would ask to be let out of the wagon before going into town. And he refused. He would insist they stay in the wagon till there.

Hoover carts: I remember the Hoover carts in our little farming community. It was a two-wheeled cart, usually had tires and hitched to a mule or ox. There weren't many of those in my community, but I do remember seeing them. And they named them the Hoover cart because Hoover was the president when the Depression started and they blamed him for the economic condition, so they called them the Hoover carts.

I have read *To Kill a Mockingbird* several times since then. And I always find something different that impresses me when I read it again.

It has meant so much to Monroeville and to the county, because it brings tourists, and our play has become a big event. I think now we're appreciating that aspect of it.

I think because we've become more aware of how unfair the system was back then before integration, that there just was no justice. Blacks did not serve on juries. Women didn't serve on juries. I think we have grown that much that now we understand how unfair the system was, how unusual it was for Atticus to take a case like that, when, as he said—and that was one of my favorite passages—when you know you can't win, but you take it anyway.

Scott Turow

Scott Turow was born in Chicago in 1949. He is a lawyer and the author of nine novels, including Presumed Innocent (1987), Personal Injuries (1999), Limitations (2006), and Innocent (2010) and two nonfiction books, One L (1997) and Ultimate Punishment: A Lawyer's Reflections on Dealing with the Death Penalty (2003).

I was pretty close to Scout's age when I read *To Kill a Mocking-bird*. It was this big best-selling novel. Probably my mother encouraged me to read it. I was enthralled by it. I loved Scout and was intensely identified with her, and in a way that, in retrospect, probably should have been more uncomfortable for a boy, but which really was not.

It was just one of those books that sucks you in and carries you along. And, of course, it was telling a story about the South that a Northern boy wanted to hear. I suppose I had lots of reasons for loving it as much as I did. One was this greatly idealized father, which, in candor, I didn't have. I was hip on race as a very young kid, which led to quite a bit of activity in the civil rights movement until white people were basically thrown out when Dr. King was killed. There was a lot of stuff in there that spoke to me. I loved the book.

I have a memory of trying to read *Anatomy of a Murder*, which was [published] a few years before, and I couldn't get through that. I did many years later with great pleasure. *To Kill a Mock-ingbird* might have been the first adult novel that I read, although I read *The Count of Monte Cristo* when I was ten, and that truly ignited my interest in what I'll call literature.

I feel constrained to talk about it a lot because *To Kill a Mock-ingbird* is a story about a lawyer. I just think the grace of the writing is substantial, and I am confounded by people who attack it as a work of literature. I think it is a beautifully written and structured book. Is it sentimental? Yes, it's sentimental, but so was Steinbeck, and people still read Steinbeck, and as my dear friend Mitch Albom [author of *Tuesdays with Morrie*] is proving, people like sentimentality. One of the things I dislike intensely about the high-art-versus-low-art people is the fact that the high-art people do not acknowledge that all stories are models of the world. It is not as if *Ulysses* didn't come with its own set of prejudices and conventions that, in point of fact, don't match "reality" as we currently apprehend it either. To attack a work because it is sentimental is not to recognize, frankly, why sentiment continues to appeal. It appeals because people want to believe in an idealized world, and that has an instructive function, an instructive moral function. It's true that there aren't many human beings in the world like Atticus Finch—perhaps none—but that doesn't mean that it's not worth striving to be like him.

I said that that certainly was the way it resonated. He is a paragon beyond paragons. In latter years, my interest in him has been that he is emblematic of the way lawyers were represented up till probably the 1980s, when all of a sudden—it was the hangover of Watergate—people realized that lawyers are not paragons. Lawyers, in some cases, are greedy scum-sucking pigs, which is as one-sided and silly a picture as to imagine that they are all paragons. I am always at pains to point out that not only is Atticus this wonderful father, completely intuitive and caring, but he is even the best shot in the county. He is everything and, of course, the only lawyer in town who will defend this black man accused of this supposedly horrible crime. He is a paragon. He is a type that Americans would no longer believe in much as a lawyer in our popular fiction of today, but that doesn't mean it's not a great book.

After *Presumed Innocent* and especially *The Burden of Proof*, I became a part-time lawyer. And one of the things that I maintained in my practice was this commitment to doing pro bono work. If you say to me, "Well, why did you want to do pro bono work?" I can't say it was Atticus alone, but certainly if you can ask me for the earliest example that I was aware of, that was it. I promised myself that when I grew up and I was a man, I would try to do things just as good and noble as what Atticus had done for Tom Robinson. So I don't think it inspired me to be a lawyer, but certainly, as a vision of the positives that lawyers can do, it did. I would be unfair to my profession if I did not add that there are many, many, many lawyers around the United States who are still doing what Atticus did.

My connection with the movie is odd, because it was the first big job that [*To Kill a Mockingbird* producer] Alan Pakula had, and Alan ultimately directed *Presumed Innocent*. Alan talked about *To Kill a Mockingbird* incessantly. The movie did not have the impact on me that the book had had. If you go back to 1960, '61, '62, when the movie finally came out, the movies were not recognized as an art at that time. They were kind of celluloid trash, and the assumption was that any movie made from any book was a lesser work, and that was the assumption in my house. I don't think I took it as seriously.

One reason the book endures is because of what I've referred to as wingspan. It can still be read by thirteen-year-olds. It can be read by blue-haired ladies and men with callused hands. It's not a hard book to read. It's a very graceful book. I think, a really moving book, and it also tells a tale that we know is still true. We may live eventually in a world where that kind of race prejudice is unimaginable, and people may read this story in three hundred years and go, "So what was the big deal?" But the fact of the matter is, in today's America, it still speaks a fundamental truth.

People understand not only that this happened, but that it still happens, and that people are falsely accused, that race is a factor. So there is a kernel of it that is very contemporary.

I cannot imagine what drove [Harper Lee] into silence, although Hemingway said that all writers really tell one story, so maybe she felt she told the story she had to tell. I don't know. It's a frightening thing to another novelist to see somebody write a book that good and then shut up. It is a great puzzle.

This was a very brave book to have written when Harper Lee wrote it, and she probably gets zero credit anymore. We are speaking a truth that people in 1959, 1960, were not ready to acknowledge. People forgot how divided this country was, what the animosity was to the Civil Rights Act, which probably never would have been passed if John F. Kennedy hadn't been assassinated, and instead it became his legacy. But that was 1963, and in 1960, there were no laws guaranteeing that African Americans could enter any restaurant, any hotel. We didn't have those laws. In that world, to speak out this way was remarkable.

Oprah Winfrey

Oprah Winfrey was born in Kosciusko, Mississippi, in 1954. She is a talk-show host, TV and film producer, founder of O, The Oprah Magazine, radio programmer, actress, philanthropist, and chairman of Harpo, Inc. Winfrey was the recipient of the National Book Foundation's Medal of Distinguished Contribution to American Letters in 1999.

*A*t the time that I read *To Kill a Mockingbird*, I was living with my mother in Milwaukee. I would not have had any money to buy it, so I would undoubtedly have chosen it from the library. I was one of those kids who would go to the library every two weeks, withdraw five books, read the five books, and return them. It was a librarian who said, "If you like reading that kind of book, I think you will like reading this book."

So I picked up *To Kill a Mockingbird* at the library. It was one of five other books, and I remember starting it and just devouring it, not being able to get enough of it, because I fell in love with Scout. I wanted to be Scout. I thought I was Scout. I always took on or wanted to take on the characteristics of whoever I was reading about, and so I wanted to be Scout and I wanted a father like Atticus.

Atticus isn't even real, I know, but my gosh, did I want a dad like Atticus! And I wanted to have a relationship like Scout had with Atticus, so I could call him by his first name. I wanted a nickname like Scout's. I was drawn to the book because of that, and it wasn't until I saw the book transformed into a film that I came to realize the depth of the racial implications of the book.

I remember watching the movie with my father many years after I first read the book. The impact of the movie on my father caused me to see the book differently and experience the book differently. I am right after the cusp of the civil rights movement. I wasn't a child of the civil rights movement. I am one of those people who has been one of the greatest beneficiaries of the civil rights movement. I don't know what it is like to be told to go to the back door.

I did not live a Jim Crow segregated life, because I was one of the fortunate ones who were able to escape Mississippi. And I do mean escape—1960, when this book was published, was about the time I was leaving Mississippi.

I left for Milwaukee and left my grandmother when I was six years old, so I never experienced the segregation of the South. I moved to an integrated school and was the smartest kid in the class, and when you are the smartest kid in the class, you always get a lot of attention. I never felt any of the oppressiveness of racism. I always recognize that life would have been so different for me had I been raised in a segregated environment, if I had to experience even secondhand what was happening in that environment.

I think of myself as a Southerner. My roots are Southern. Not only was I born in the South, in Mississippi, but for a great part of my life, I was raised in Tennessee, so I identify with being a Southern woman.

I identified with being a Southern child. After reading this book, I wished I had an accent, and I would go around trying to imitate Scout. It was really sickening, I guess. I scared a lot of other kids because, just like I do now, I remember reading this book and then going to class and not being able to shut up about it. I read it in eighth or ninth grade, and I was trying to push the book off on other kids. So it makes sense to me that now I have a book club, because I have been doing that since probably this book. This is one of the first books I wanted to encourage other people to read.

I loved it from the beginning, and like a lot of people, I get the lines blurred between the movie and the book. The movie is very distinct for me because the reading experience comes alive for me in a way that my imagination cannot. In the history of film-making I have never seen a book really live its essence through film like this one, and that is because of the casting of Scout and Atticus, and all of them, really.

Maybe ten years ago, I had the honor of being seated next to Gregory Peck at a luncheon held for Quincy Jones in Hollywood. I was so like, *Oh my God, it is Gregory Peck. What I am going to do? What I am going say? I am not just at the same table, but next to Gregory Peck.* Even though it is long after I have had the talk show and I have interviewed many people, I could not think of one thing to say. Finally I turned and I said, "So, how is Scout doing?" And he said, "Well, that was forty years ago, but OK." I say, "So, how is Scout doing? Do you ever see her?" Because in my brain, no matter what role Gregory Peck has done since then, he will always be Atticus to me, and whoever the woman was who played Scout is, she is always Scout in my mind.

You just liked Scout. You connected with her. I liked her energy. I liked the spirit of her. I liked the freshness of her. I liked the fact that she was so curious. I loved this character so much. The character was so fully realized and showed, even at ten years old, that she knew who she was and was very assertive and had a lot of confidence and believed in herself and was learning about this whole world of racism in such a way that I could feel myself also experiencing or learning about it—my eyes opening as her eyes were opening to it.

I think *To Kill a Mockingbird* is our national novel. If there was a national novel award, this would be it for the United States. I think it is a favorite book of almost everybody you meet. When I opened my school [in South Africa], everybody wanted to know what we can bring and what can we give the girls. I asked everybody to bring their favorite book, and I would say we probably have a hundred copies of this book. Each person who brought the book wrote their own words to the girls about why they believe this book was important, and everybody says something different.

Of course I wanted to choose this for the book club even though America already loves it. I thought, "Wouldn't it be an amazing thing to have Harper Lee come on and be interviewed for *To Kill a Mockingbird*?" I started that process several years ago and worked on it for a couple of years with my staff calling back and forth between her agent.

Finally, we were able to arrange a meeting, and I was so excited. I remember it was a rainy day in New York, and we were going to have lunch at the Four Seasons. I saw her walking along the street with an umbrella and boots. It was so disarming and charming I couldn't believe it. So all of that *What am I going to say? What am I going to do?* went away. We were like instant girlfriends. It was just wonderful, and I loved being with her. I knew twenty minutes into the conversation that I would never be able to convince her to do an interview, and it is not my style to push. I decided to relax and enjoy this time that I had. Because [in Southern accent] honey, she was not going to be convinced at all. She said to me, "I already said everything I needed to say. Already we have those buses coming down to my house, and they pull up to the door still looking for Boo Radley, and I just don't want that to happen any more than it already does." She said no, and I knew that no meant no. Sometimes no means, "Hmm . . . let us see what else you have to say." But when Harper Lee said, "Well, honey, I already said everything I had to say," I knew that was the end of it. I just enjoyed the lunch. It was fantastic.

I think, *Why didn't I take a tape recorder?* because your brain is like, *Oh my God, oh my God, oh my God, I am having lunch with Harper Lee, and I hope I remember everything, and I am trying to memorize every sentence she is saying!* Then afterwards you say, "What did she say? What did I say?"

One of the things that struck me: She said, "If I had a dime for every book that was sold . . ." *I was thinking, I hope you have more than a dime for every book that was sold, because nobody expected this.* Certainly she didn't expect it, and obviously the publishers didn't expect it. [Fifty years later], we are still talking about this book and that it is the number one book on almost everybody in America's list for their favorite novel. So she wasn't prepared for it.

She said to me, "You know the character Boo Radley?" And she said, "Well, if you know Boo, then you understand why I wouldn't be doing an interview, because I am really Boo." That is all she had to say to me. OK, I know we are not going to bring Boo Radley out to sit on the *Oprah* show.

I was honored to be able to have that time and communicate with her. That was very special, and I take it for what it is. She will be one of those people, like Jackie Onassis, who I also had wanted to interview, who told me no, and I honor that.

The way I felt about being turned down is exactly the way I felt about Jackie Onassis. In the end, I was glad that she didn't do it, that she was able to hold on to that for herself. I believe [Harper Lee] is never going to do an interview, and I am glad that she didn't. I am glad that she was able to hold on to that, because she is obviously a woman of great principles and integrity.

Andrew Young

Andrew Young was born in 1932 in New Orleans. He has been the United States ambassador to the United Nations, a congressman from Georgia, and was the mayor of Atlanta from 1982 to 1990. Young was a minister who joined the Southern Christian Leadership Conference in 1960 and worked closely with Martin Luther King Jr.

I wasn't much of a fiction reader. I read encyclopedias. I read weird stuff. I didn't sit down and read books until I was getting a little older. But I remember Atticus Finch. For me, he represents a generation of intelligent white lawyers who eventually, in the fifties and sixties, became the federal judges who changed the South.

We didn't know very many white people of principle when I was a child—not any who were willing to stand up and challenge the system in any way. When I was in seminary, I worked for Adlai Stevenson. Then I came south to Georgia. Thomasville, Georgia, was my first church, and the black leadership had asked me to run a voter registration drive to encourage people to vote for Eisenhower. And I said, "Why?" And they said, "Well, everywhere else it might not be the same, but if Eisenhower wins, he will appoint judges that are men of integrity and the most intelligent people in the South. And he will listen to us. We will have some input. The Democrats to be appointed are really Dixiecrats. And they're the old segregationists." So, for Georgia in 1956, Eisenhower was my choice. And he didn't let us down. Later on in the sixties, we marched from Selma to Montgomery in large measure to get to the court of Judge Frank Johnson—not that he was liberal, but he was fair. He believed in the Constitution.

In Saint Augustine, Florida, in '64 they tried to beat us up, and the sheriff deputized the Ku Klux Klan and gave them permission to beat us. It was Judge Brian Simpson, another Eisenhower appointee, who upheld the Constitution and protected us and our right to march. And that helped to bring about the passage of the 1964 Civil Rights Act.

In school desegregation cases in New Orleans, it was Judge

Minor Wisdom. In Atlanta it was Judge Griffin Bell and Judge Elbert Tuttell. These were all the Southern intelligentsia—and they were Atticus Finch. They were the fine, upstanding men of wisdom and courage that really—without them we would not have had a civil rights movement.

To Kill a Mockingbird is like *Gone with the Wind*. It describes an era of history that we know about glibly. But it gives us a sense of emerging humanism and decency. About that same time, or a little earlier, it was W. J. Cash, *The Mind of the South*, which talked about people pitting the races against each other because they were both poor.

Another book was *The Strange Career of Jim Crow*. We were aware of the harshness and brutality of segregation. In Birmingham, you had for the first time black people making union wages in the steel mills. And they began to build nice homes. Now these were veterans of service in the military who came back, went to school, got good jobs, and started building nice little homes—nothing fancy, just little three-bedroom frame houses. And there were more than sixty of those houses dynamited before we came to change the civil rights movement.

To Kill a Mockingbird gave us the background of that. But it also gave us hope that justice could prevail. I think that's one of the things that makes it a great story—it can be repeated in many different ways. I was always surprised at how much the Japanese liked *Gone with the Wind*. But they liked the fact that this society had been destroyed by war and was reborn. And they identified their destruction and their resurrection with *Gone with the Wind*.

I think *To Kill a Mockingbird* does that for the sixties. But the conditions that created it, still to this day in 2009, exist in some parts of the Middle East, Africa, China, India, also in some parts of Europe and America. It's not the legal injustices that we talked about in *To Kill a Mockingbird* [that] still exist today.

There's a whole genre of police shows—*CSI, Cold Case, Law & Order*—and I find myself looking at them because quite often they're about people who are victims of injustice [in] one way or the other. And for the most part, justice prevails. We need to see that. We need to believe that in order to keep the society together. *To Kill a Mockingbird* is a book that inspires hope in the midst of chaos and confusion. And those kinds of books last for a long time.

[The use of the word *nigger*] is not something that is even resolved in the black community. I always used it as a term of affection and admiration. That's not the way white people tended to use it. But I think it's like any word. It's not the word itself, it's the intent and meaning of the word. I would say that is one of the great dangers of our public schools and our reactionary society. I heard that somebody wanted to ban Maya Angelou's *I Know Why the Caged Bird Sings*. Now that is the reality of her life. *To Kill a Mockingbird* was the reality of that time. I don't think it makes us any wiser or smarter to deny that.

I can't read Richard Wright. That's too cruel. I had a hard time struggling through *Roots*. I read *The Diary of Anne Frank*, and I read a little of the existentialism that came out of the Holocaust. But the big books on the Holocaust I couldn't deal with emotionally. They made me too bitter. And that may be why I did not read *To Kill a Mockingbird*. I didn't need to read that. I knew what they were talking about. For somebody who didn't know, OK. But I had no intellectual curiosity about that. I had been through that with my life. I had been through that with my father, and my grandfather. It was too close to me. I remember Emmett Till and all of that drama around that. I was a part of the march around Jimmy Lee Jackson's death. And the three civil rights workers, Schwerner, Goodman, and Chaney. There was too much horror around me at the time for me to absorb more.

Now I think, though, it's different. Young people need to look back and realize how far we've come but how the seeds of that same insecurity still exist.

To Kill a Mockingbird was an act of protest, but it was [also] an act of humanity.

It was saying that we're not all like this. There are people who rise above their prejudices and even above the law.

Acknowledgments

This all started on my back porch when I reread *To Kill a Mockingbird* for the *third* time. I was looking for solace and found it. After that came inspiration. And then, my good friends and colleagues fueled me forward.

Connie Hays, from my girlhood summers, was first. A pithy purveyor of good instructions for life—how to coddle an egg for Caesar salad, interview a recalcitrant police sergeant, talk to your boss without crying, quell a child's tantrum—Connie was certain I should do this. And, as it always was with us, her confidence gave me confidence. Connie was kind and funny and brave. She left us entirely too soon and with no instructions for how to get along without her. I miss her all the time and I dedicate this project to her.

This never would have happened without the incredibly talented and generous Rich White, a magnificent director of photography. Cathleen McGuigan, my *Newsweek* officemate in the eighties and friend ever since, kept my confidences and helped pave the way for me in places where I needed it most. Don Hewitt, once my boss at *60 Minutes,* greeted this idea with his usual gusto and had nothing short of a zillion suggestions. His infectious enthusiasm in the early stages was heartening for me, and I am sorry he is not here to see this.

A salute to the Ladies' Auxiliary: Rosanne Cash, Adriana

Acknowledgments

Trigiani, Jenny Baldwin, Taylor Barton, Sheilah Crowley, Sheila Berger, Wren Arthur, Jane Martin, and Liz Tirrell. What began as a festive annual lunch has brought year-round sustenance and solidarity for more than a decade. On the subject of great women: Sarah Crichton sent me a letter I will never, ever, forget, and Kathy McManus gave me a leg up when I needed one.

I am grateful to all the people I interviewed, especially Wally Lamb.

Many thanks to Elizabeth Buerger and Romy Feder for research, to my former *60 Minutes* colleague Bryony Kockler, who lent her considerable skills to the project; and to Megan Axthelm Brown, a fantastic production manager and a remarkable person.

Many more friends and colleagues heard me out, spurred me on, and gave me valuable feedback: Ben Cheever and Janet Maslin, Jennifer and Craig Whitaker, Frank Delaney and Diane Meier, Bob Mayer and Edie Magnus, Joan Jakobson, John Hays, Lynn Rabren and Joanne McDonough, Jane Beasley, Doreen Schechter, Tony Hoyt, Esther Kartiganer, Sarah Callahan Zusi, Mike Whitney, Cathy Lasiewicz, Ellen Hale, Pete Bonventre, Chris Seward, Gail Marowitz, Lisa Linden, Mary Dolan, Lynn Goldberg, Jon Alter, Chloe Arensberg, Chip Logan, Amanda Lundberg, Kari Granville and Peter Boyer, Charles Kaiser and Joe Stouter, Betsy West, Marilyn and Michael Seymour, Julie and Carol Kalberer, Tina Hester and Bob Garrett.

When it came time to turn everything into a book, agent Richard Pine made the experience positively dreamy, editor Hugh Van Dusen was a true gentleman, and assistant editor Rob Crawford was a patient guide to the process. My thanks to Jarrod Taylor for his elegant design and to Kate Blum for manning the publicity barricades.

Acknowledgments

There have been no greater friends to this book, or to me, than Hal Fessenden and Pat Eisemann, two people well schooled in the ins and outs of publishing. Their knowledge, support, and advice were indispensable throughout, as has been their friendship, humor, and original thinking.

Josh Howard and Debbie DeLuca Sheh are two people you want in your foxhole and on the next barstool. My 911s and 411s in life go to Emily Lazar, the Honorable Jen Laird White, and Saint Judith Tygard of Sleepy Hollow, and I am so much better because of them.

Two smart friends and neighbors, author Marilyn Johnson and editor Janet Pietsch, gave the manuscript a careful, constructive read as I sprinted toward the finish line, and it made all the difference.

My mother and sister, Susan and Martha Murphy, who know a lot about books, are the reason I read *To Kill a Mockingbird* in the first place. For this, their spirited company in life, and much more, I am very thankful. And, by the way, Mom, I do not hate your cooking. Thanks to my brothers, Dan and Patrick, for being on my side; sister and brother-in-law, Emily and Mark; and to my Murphy, Seymour, and McDonagh relatives—it's a great tribe.

A champagne toast to my father, Ray Murphy: I am grateful, more than I can say, for his faith and trust in me. Not everyone has her own Atticus, but I do. My in-house editors, young Kate and James Minzesheimer, make anyone's disposition sunnier, especially mine. And then there is Bob, a man of red sneakers and great perspective. Without his love, loyalty, and understanding, there would be none of the above.

Illustration credits

Grateful acknowledgment is made for permission to reprint the photographs on the following pages:

11   Harper Lee, flanked by C-SPAN founder Brian Lamb and Ellen Johnson Sirleaf, the president of Liberia, recipients of the Presidential Medal of Freedom, November 5, 2007. Courtesy of Alex Wong/Getty Images News.

19   Harper Lee poses for *Life* magazine in the balcony of the old courthouse in Monroeville, Alabama, May 1961. Courtesy of Donald Uhrbrock/Time & Life Pictures/Getty Images.

21   Monroeville Courthouse. Courtesy of Monroe County Heritage Museum.

22   Amasa Coleman Lee, Harper Lee's father. Courtesy of Monroe County Heritage Museum.

22   Frances Finch Lee, Harper Lee's mother. Courtesy of Monroe County Heritage Museum.

24   Young Truman Capote with his aunt in Monroeville, Alabama. Courtesy of Monroe County Heritage Museum.

27   Advertisement for *To Kill a Mockingbird*, 1960.

33   Mary Badham as Scout in the film of *To Kill a Mockingbird*. Courtesy of Mary Badham Wilt.